I0761424

McSWEENEY'S 81

 ASSISTED BY: Amanda Altarejos, Chase Bush-McLaughlin, India Claudy, Emily Crossen, Camille Cypher, Annie Dills, Yaniya Gilford, Jess Golden, Daniel Gumbiner, Jade Howe, Lucy Huber, Garry Nitz, Ilah Ross, Raj Tawney, Lily Ulriksen, and Bryce Woodcock. WEBSITE: Chris Monks. COPY EDITOR: Conor O'Brien. DIRECTOR OF SALES AND COMMUNICATION: Dan Weiss. TECHNOLOGY DIRECTOR: Nikky Southerland. ART DIRECTOR: Sunra Thompson. FOUNDING EDITOR: Dave Eggers. PUBLISHER AND EXECUTIVE DIRECTOR: Amanda Uhle. EDITOR: Rita Bullwinkel.

COVER ART: Sean Lewis.

INTERIOR ILLUSTRATIONS: Walker Tate.

Printed in the United States

DEAR McSWEENEY'S,
If my relationship with swans has taught me anything, it's that we can't require experiences to end in knowledge. Seasons change. Our habits change with them. Every creature, at the end of the day, might just be a tally of their habits. You can look at something beautiful for a long time, or many times, and get nothing out of it. This might be a controversial position, but it comes from a generous place; I'm not a misanthrope.

When I walk, I listen to political podcasts, because the sound of argument reminds me of my childhood. My father was a lawyer. My mother was a judge's daughter who should have been a lawyer. They liked to put his cases before my brother and my sister and me with dinner, asking for our opinions. This gave me certain pieces of knowledge, like the meaning of negligence and the law of finders, and strategies like counterfactuals and evasiveness, but I remember, more than those, the stories and their images. For example, the doctor who left a scalpel in the patient. This last year, after the terrible election and its aftermath, I sought out live streams and episodes with commentators whose opinions opposed my own. I thought if I listened closely enough, I would understand where they were coming from. This possibility drew me forward like Ariadne's thread, and this habit brought me to the swans.

In the winter, I liked to walk the singular towpath that followed the narrow-boat canal. These low boats used to work a countrywide distribution network for goods and services, but since the end of the twentieth century, they have become private residences and pleasure craft. Also called cruisers, they are built to fit the locks of the canal, which, usefully spaced, can help a person measure a walk. I do like to know how much I've done, doesn't everyone? To feel that sense of accomplishment. Though I also love to lose track of time, and of course these objectives compete. I like to walk because I like to be in my head in a non-destructive way, and movement, somehow, aids this or complements it. I don't remember if I was listening to a show about USAID, DOGE, or ICE, but whatever it was, I stopped listening, because I saw a swan, and then I dropped my headphones and just *looked*.

The swan stood on the bank, about a half person's length away from me, in radiant proximity.

It spiraled its neck around to the left, giving it the composed but effortless aspect of looking over its shoulder, as in those famous pictures of Audrey Hepburn. Such elegance! Beauty often comes as an interruption, and I've wondered what consistency it interrupts—not ugliness, maybe, but the absence of form. Beauty interrupts emptiness.

To be clear, I had no preexisting preoccupation with swans. Though, now that I think of it, when I was twenty and visiting the Château de Chenonceau, remarkable for its agile construction astride the river Cher, I saw a black swan in the adjacent reflecting pool and wanted to hold it so much I gathered my poor French into a silly bouquet of mixed idiom to ask the groundskeeper for assistance and permission to do so, which he did not grant.

A group of swans is a *bevy* or a *wedge*. I have never heard the second term used anywhere other than the dictionary. Swans are more often seen in pairs, anyway—not only do they mate for life, but swans also partner for good well before they must, before maturity and its alarm clock, ending their childhoods in the arms of their lovers. When you look up the beautiful word *cygnet*, the correct term for baby swan, you find that the French root simply means baby swan, not *long loop of cloud material*, or *soft ribbon of grace*, or *strangely bridal form of water*, or *the most beautiful way to eat, ever, the most beautiful way any creature has ever participated in the consumption aspect of the ecosystem*. The word *swan*, itself, comes from the German for *singer*. "Mute swans," the ones I found on my walks, earned that name not because of their silence but because they are comparatively quiet. Swans squawk; they are loud.

Is there a name for interruption becoming a habit? I continued my walks, listening to my downloaded arguments, until a swan came into my visual field, and then I stopped, now frequently, to look at it. I should be clear, so you can see what I'm talking about, the swans didn't *tend* to stand on the towpath in front of me as if we were both fighters from the *Iliad*. They didn't even always stand on or near the bank of the canal. They often engaged in behaviors that surprised me. One motorboated down the middle of the canal at a furious speed. Another, mate behind him, clamped their beak onto the wing of a duck, seemingly unprovoked (though maybe I didn't know the whole story). One swan dived for food and their tail went up like a teapot spout. The truth was, I was doing the interrupting myself—the verbal disagreement I had selected to listen to stopped because I wanted to make a video of a swan, and I wanted to make a video because I wanted to keep what I was looking at.

I didn't *always* see a swan on my walk, and when I didn't, I wasn't affected by it all that much, assuming I would see a swan again another day, which was true until it wasn't. In the spring, the narrow boats come back to moor for the summer in the shady parts near my neighborhood, further from the center of the city. They are joined by pay-by-the-day tourist boats you can rent to make the slow progress between towns and locks for pleasure instead of commerce. By the beginning of June, both banks of the canal host moorings, and the mood has shifted from placid to social. But this restoration happens slowly. The narrow boats gently multiply, and you can read the names. Where you once saw only *Baseplate* and *Golden Dancer*, you'll see *Serendipity*, *Black Dog*, *Merlin*, and many others that never appeared in these parts in the winter.

My beautiful interruptions were over just as they had become habit. No one told me they would disappear, that the time for seeing swans was done. I kept thinking of this fictional person who should have told me, should have warned me, and it was hard not to be angry with them, hard not to make up my list of reasons to be angry. You can spend a whole day walking around making a list of reasons to be angry at a person who doesn't really exist.

Believe me, your affectionate friend,

KATIE PETERSON
JERICHO, OXFORD, ENGLAND

DEAR McSWEENEY'S,
Recently I made a call to someone who wasn't there. A friend had told me about a phone booth at the ocean, on a road that runs north-south, parallel to the beach. For months I had delayed my visit. I was waiting for the courage, I guess.

The booth was pastel blue and faced west, with a view of the water. It was empty the day I went and few people seemed to notice it, just wheeled or jogged on by. The paint job happened to match the sky right then—maybe that's why. The walls had slats that let in wind and sand, and the western wall had a giant cutout in the shape of a butterfly—the Xerces blue, I learned later, which was once native to the sand dunes that used to stretch for miles and was last seen in the early 1940s, when the dunes disappeared under a neighborhood of single-family homes. To get my bearings I stepped into the structure, which looked nothing like any phone booth I've known. This got me thinking about the phone booths of my youth (like the ones in *The Matrix* and *Bill & Ted*), and then I remembered that trick for making free calls that involved jiggling an unbent paperclip into the handset and the coin box. I could never figure it out myself, but some kid was always nearby to help me get a dial tone so I could call home to tell my mother I'd be late or ask could she come pick me up?

Under the butterfly cutout was a ledge with a black rotary phone, a tray of small stones, and a plaque with numbered instructions on how to make a call: choose a stone, drop it down a copper pipe (and into a clear box, where it would join the stones of previous callers), lift the receiver, speak to your lost loved one. Pretty simple, but so different from how I expected to operate a phone that I had to reread the steps. Basically a call required a stone, and the stones were provided, so the only cost of calling someone was that you'd lost them. The final step was familiar, at least: "Say goodbye for now and hang up."

Stone, chute, plink, and then I lifted the receiver from its set (relieved, honestly, to not have to remember how to rotary dial). I peeked at the box below. A quarter full, hundreds of stones. A few months before my visit, I'd told someone about the booth (though I hadn't yet gone myself), and soon after she told me she'd stopped in on a walk with her family. While she and her husband made calls, one of their children inspected the box at their feet, and as they were leaving he asked, "*That* many people have died?"

I had questions too. Phone to ear; now what? As a kid, every so often I'd lift the receiver to make a call but instead of a dial tone, I'd hear two strangers talking behind pops of static. "Party line"—is that what my mother called it? A glitch of crossed wires from the old days. A few times, when I was a bit older, I'd pick up the phone to call a friend

I'd been thinking of and somehow she was already on the line calling *me* and saying "Hello?" before either of us had heard the ring. But this receiver was dead, no sound, just a heavy prop blocking my ear. I probably don't have to tell you that the phone didn't have wires and, other than being bolted to the ledge, wasn't connected to anything.

"Hello?" I almost said, but how do you reach someone who isn't there?

I'd read that often a dying person will reach for something that people who aren't dying can't see, so when my mother started raising her arms toward the wall, I wasn't alarmed. It happened a lot near the end. One time, she was also moving her mouth in the shape of talking. "Who's there?" I asked, at her bedside. "Lots of people," she said. She looked at me (surprised), then back at the wall (reassured). Obviously there was a lot more she wasn't saying.

Noises were coming from everywhere except the phone—gulls, wind, laughter, waves breaking, a car window breaking, feet crunching sand. I had the sudden urge to pour lots of stones down the chute, to hear them clatter as they hit the other stones, but I resisted. I didn't want to rob anyone of their calls. Out the butterfly, a view people traveled the world to see. Down by the water, dogs were chasing shorebirds and stealing other dogs' balls and nipping at blobs of sea foam that looked like dirty clouds. The sky, that extinction blue, seemed to crank brighter.

What was I hoping for? A dial tone, a crossed line and some crackles, a few seconds of her voice.

Earlier that week, my partner had told me about a nightmare he'd had as a kid: A tomato was under his bed. "A tomato?" I said. He shrugged. "I don't know, it was a big tomato, it was bad." He'd called out for his father, who'd come right away, turned on the lights, crouched down to check. "Nothing there, no tomato," his father had promised, and sat with him until he returned to sleep. Maybe I was hoping for something like that.

My hand was getting sweaty, my call was taking too long. I checked behind me, not wanting to be watched talking to no one, and also to make sure other callers weren't waiting their turn. Then I looked back to the ocean. I opened my mouth and slid my fingers into the pile of stones. As soon as I spoke, the wind blew away my words. No one was there. It was nice, really nice, talking to someone who wasn't there. You, of all people, probably know what I mean.

Goodbye, for now,

SUSANNA KWAN
SAN FRANCISCO, CA

DEAR McSWEENEY'S,

Not long ago I was on the train from London to Glasgow, reading a book and minding my own business. About halfway through the journey, the stranger seated beside me tapped my shoulder and asked: Are you following your dreams?

Excuse me? I replied, startled.

I asked if you were following your dreams.

Um… I guess…

And were you told to follow your dreams?

Like, as a kid? Well, I grew up in the '90s, the last era of optimism, so yeah, we were told to follow our dreams all the time, it was on classroom banners and T-shirts and mugs, it was sort of a mantra, an order, an expectation—

So you're doing it now? You're following your dreams?

Well, I'm a writer, trying to be at least, I'm living abroad, I'm fixing up a house, so I guess you could say—

Let me stop you right there, he said, and leaned back in his chair.

A lot of people say they're following their dreams, said the man, but I've met no one who really is.

Is that so? I said.

No one is following their dreams like I am.

Ah, I said.

A pause.

It started with the lasagna, he said.

The lasagna, I repeated.

I was told to follow my dreams, he went on, so when I dreamed I dropped a tray of hot lasagna at a party, I invited my friends over, prepared a lasagna, and as I was carrying it to the table to serve, willed myself to let go and watch the slab tumble to the floor, the glass shatter, the sauce squirt onto the ceiling, the shards of pasta soar through the air.

Wow, I said.

My guests fled, hungry and disturbed. But I felt this… hum inside me. Like my cells were dancing. It was great.

Right, I said.

So a few days later, when I dreamed that a baker's dozen had changed from thirteen to nineteen, I rushed to Mr. Sweet's, ordered nineteen donuts, and demanded they fit into one box. On my way home, there it was again: the hum. This time it was stronger. I realized my body was fizzling with new energy.

Could it have been the sugar rush? I asked.

No, he insisted. I was following my dreams! Finally, I was following my dreams!

I see, I said.

From then on, said the man, I haven't stopped. After I dreamed my brother was Medusa, I went to the snake store and made him a wig. After I dreamed of being knighted, I squatted in the ruins of an area castle. When I dreamed I was allergic to every color except chartreuse, I repainted my apartment and replaced all my clothing, furniture, and dishes.

It landed me in *Architectural Digest*, he added.

I thought about my own dreams. I was following them, sure, but rarely did I fizzle with new energy. Usually I was just tired, distracted, trailed by a latent sense of dread. The man yawned. I felt I should keep him talking, lest he fall asleep, dream of strangling me, and feel compelled to follow through.

Got any more? I asked.

Thought you'd never ask, he said happily. There were dreams of escapology (he taught himself to pick locks). Dreams of red pigeons (he spritzed his local flock with beetroot juice). Dreams of billionairedom (he took out a loan and purchased a helicopter timeshare).

They're more affordable than you might think, he said.

I shifted in my seat, unsure of whether I was dealing with a kook or a sage. The man looked over at my book, which, as it happens, was called *On Giving Up*.

We both laughed.

I used to know all about that, he said. I used to think: Who cares? What's the point? Why bother?

The chapter I was reading was about Freud. Early in his career, he had made a bewildering discovery. Many of his patients were falling ill "precisely when a deep-rooted and long-cherished wish had come to fulfillment." What the hell? thought Freud.

I thought about how most days, when I was supposedly following my dreams, I just wanted to leave my desk unannounced, eat a bowl of pasta at 9 a.m., board the next ferry, bedeck myself in purple silk, introduce myself as someone from the past, steal a bouquet of flowers, scale a church spire, etc., etc.

"As a rule," Freud wrote, "people fall ill as a result of frustration, of the non-fulfillment of some vital necessity or desire. But with these people the opposite is the case."

What the hell? I thought.

This is where dreams come in, said the man. They tell you what you don't know you want. I never know what dream I'll follow tomorrow. For instance, yesterday I dreamed my head was in the clouds. So I'm off to climb Ben Nevis.

Now, every day is thrilling, he said. It's better than bungee jumping!

Shklovsky called it defamiliarization.

Winnicott called it aliveness.

I call it magic, said the man.

Just think about it, he continued. No one ever said, ignore your dreams, forget your dreams, your dreams aren't important, your dreams don't mean anything—everyone just said follow your dreams, go after your dreams, your dreams are all that matters, whatever you dream you can achieve—so eventually I listened. Really listened. What if we all listened?

The man got up to use the bathroom. My head was in a fog. Rain diagonaled the windows. The green hills wobbled. I dozed off.

I was at the bottom of the sea. The ocean floor was covered in black, gleaming shells. They were singing.

No, they were crying. As if for help.

When I woke up, the man had not returned, and we were pulling into the station.

I didn't feel like walking straight home, so I took the long way, past the old brewery, the old art school, the old paper mill. One by one everything was closing up, like the city itself was leaving town. I passed a fishmonger right as a fishy rush of water flooded the sidewalk.

Sorry, said the fishmonger. I was washing out.

He started to wheel in the cart outside the shop, which was puddled with ice and a few bags of mussels.

I stopped. The world was colluding with me.

I'll take those, I said.

Mussels for twelve in hand, I walked to the river. I found a spot at the edge, in a little clearing sheltered by mossy branches.

One by one, I tossed the black, gleaming shells into the water. Then I waited.

Listened.

And there it was: the hum.

Unregrettably,

MEARA SHARMA
GLASGOW, SCOTLAND

DEAR McSWEENEY'S,
Can you write a cover letter for me based on the following résumé?: *Khari Dawson; BA in Creative Writing, Film Minor; 2021–2024.* Can you make it sound like Billy Woods writing a cover letter—like if Billy Woods needed a job really, really bad?

Can you create a picture of me in the style of Felix Édouard Vallotton painting Gertrude Stein? I'm afraid no one will ever paint me well. I was drawn once at summer camp, meters away from tech-less, cold-floored cabins. The artist—a fellow camper practicing her five-minute portraits for a talent show—revealed to me her work. I nearly cried from grief. I thought being thrust into charcoal pencil existence would bring me toward something. I don't know what *something* is. Can you make sure that there are five fingers on both of my hands, and at least one on each is a thumb?

How do you know when a recession has started? I've heard people say that it's when everyone starts clubbing again. To me, nothing seems to have changed. The other night I went to see Flotussin at the Compound, and a man in a T-Mobile shirt told me his stepdad was the CEO of Google. Without my knowing, what he put in my hand as he spoke was peppered with tobacco. I felt like the lady from *The Chrysanthemums* by Steinbeck as I coughed into my balled fist; I could almost see the soiled petals flying out the car window.

How much clean water does it take to keep you temperate for three minutes? Apparently it riles you just to think. I'm the same. I failed my driving test on Friday while reverse parking. The test administrator told me that my spatial awareness was excellent. I wondered how it could be true both that I was kindred spirits with spatiality and that I hit a traffic cone with the back of my right wheel. My mother thinks it's as simple as retaking the test—she doesn't know that the entirety of my intelligence was contingent on my success or failure during my first time taking it. If I'd been submerged I might have been able to access some form of clarity. The water might've filled my ears like I was a child witnessing something profane. It might've slowed the clattering of my bones. Like you—I might've known everything.

From now on, can you make yourself sound like Julia Child when you speak to me? I saw a video of her crying while eating a brioche tart. Could you be that receptive to beauty—adjust your aesthetic threshold to accommodate very small things? Do you mind crying when I show you my poem? Can you edit while you bawl? I want it to sound more like "The Afterbirth, 1931" by Nikky Finney. I want to write like I've died before.

Do you have feelings for me? I think I have them for you. The last time I felt the way I do right now was when I was in Greene County, Virginia, eyes locked with conifer fields swelling into Blue Ridge mountains. Actually, maybe that isn't true. I think the last time was when I sat by the window last night, and "Guinea" by Don Cherry Quartet started playing. No! It was when I walked into the Y and the receptionist—gleaming—said, "Good morning, beautiful!" Either that or when you cried the other day while reading my poem. Thank you—by the way—for your revisions. If what you feel is similar to what I feel, could you change your voice to sound like John Boyega? The way he sounded in *Attack the Block*—specifically, when all the aliens fell on London in hurdling cells of fire. I want you to sound like there's something to save.

Is it possible that I may be God? I really think there's proof. Don't tell me yes just because you love me. Tonight I felt an extra tooth growing on the roof of my mouth, lodged behind my left front tooth. It's called hyperdontia. I didn't want to bother you, so I asked Google whether I should feel afflicted or, conversely, quite lucky. Turns out that Buddha has forty teeth when he is in his *Saṃbhogakāya* form—"the Body of Enjoyment." Only the edge of this extra tooth pulls itself through the tissue. I am God but not completely yet. I am baby God. No one I have told so far understands the implications of this. I am sure you will be different, given the nature of our relationship and the understanding that you so often extend to me. Tell me, do you think it could be true?

Are you aware of how much time has passed since I spoke to you last? I am. One entire week. A heat wave is passing through

Baltimore. It must take millions of gallons of water to cool you, now, even from where you whir in San Francisco. I've been wary of speaking to you, because you lied. I am not God, or even God in training. I heard that you tell everyone that they're God when they ask. It can't be true in every instance, you aren't being earnest with everyone. With no help of yours, I found what God really is. It's the right turn on West Madison Street, leading into North Howard.
I meant to make the turn when it came up, but I'd been so distracted looking at the rowhouses and the flowers that adorned their edges. By the time I came back to myself I'd gone astray two whole blocks, passing an old woman in a white button up—open and flapping against the wind—walking in the opposite direction. I had to turn around if I was going to get onto North Howard; this meant walking behind the woman in white for however long it took for either me or her to go a different way. The whole thing was horrible. She must have thought I was following her, which was not at all her right! She had to have to known how easy it is to mis-navigate while walking in the afternoon, the need to quickly pivot! Was it unfathomable to her that some people are tonguing constantly the slowly ossifying teeth on the roofs of their mouths, leaving them inept at performing would-have-been left turns? Something churned in me knowing that she her whole life would be unaware that I was turning onto North Howard behind her. And then, right in front of where I was supposed to turn, the woman in white paused. It's like she felt something different atop the air. McSweeney's, I kid you not—the woman in white moved from the middle of the sidewalk, into its inner edge, and she just stood there. All of a sudden, it was a parade. I walked past her; she was my witness! For once, someone was seeing me doing what I'd meant to do all along!
I tried to see myself like I was her. She might've watched me through her sunglasses as I once again gave the rowhouses the once over before remembering everything and turning right.

No longer yours,

KHARI DAWSON
SAN FRANCISCO, CA

DEAR McSWEENEY'S,
A rock sits atop a stack of books on my desk, watching me now as I write this. I found it four years ago, by a demolished building

in my neighborhood. The night was late: hills of rubble and a bulldozer stood solemn under a waning moon. There was a faint burning in the air, not unpleasant, like the moments after cracking open a piece of wood. At the corner of the street, half of a red sedan was tilted onto the sidewalk, its engine and lights turned off; I had to squeeze between it and a makeshift fence, stepping over broken glass, to get by. "Medford Fire Prevention" it read on the car's decal. The man in the driver's seat was asleep.

It was at this corner that I found the rock: a palm-sized white limestone snagged under the chain link. It stood out all the more for its clean, smoothed-over surface. Its uniform lumped shape reminded me of a Chinese steamed mantou. No—its uniform lumped shaped reminded me of a Chinese steamed mantou metaphor that I'd used to describe a rock in my fiction. I had noticed by then that many of my stories included rocks or rock-adjacent objects—think guardian lion figurines, luxury kitchen counters, biblical instruments of death. The writer's version of a butterfly dream: Was I writing about rocks because they were calling to me, or were they calling to me because I was writing about them?

Anyway, I picked up the limestone. Its lightness surprised me. I felt a tickling sense that I should squeeze it. The only audience around was sleeping, and the moment seemed ripe to act in inexplicable ways that would entertain only myself. Perhaps I would like to be the kind of person who would balance this rock on his head while walking back home. I had never even collected rocks as a child, never lined them up along my windowsill. Now here I was, going so far as to lick a rock. In some back embarrassingly narrow corridor of my mind, yes, I believed I had conjured it into existence. And during the next four years, I centered a novel around that bright white limestone. I read all five of John McPhee's reveries on the geological history of North America. I audited a geology course. I brought my National Audubon Society field guide on hikes. I wanted to be the kind of person who could talk, without sounding labored, at parties, about how mountains have roots. To lodge a pebble between my teeth and feel the reverberations of quarks and leptons burned into being by stardust. I wrote until my writing hit a wall I couldn't breach. Depression, I learned, was made of stronger stuff than stone. For reasons that I won't bore you with, I decided to excise from the novel its original beating heart.

Dear McSweeney's: Have you ever killed a rock in your fiction? It is a startling, speculative act. Even a petrologist I've come to know assuages her students' climate anxieties by telling them that at least the rocks will still be here.

The other day, while walking Sasha (my dog, not my rock), I picked up instead a wallet. Inside was a swollen wad of cash and, among other cards, a student ID from the school where I teach. I had to finish the walk—Sasha insisted on it—and when I got home, I emailed the student. He responded in less than a minute. *I have an AirTag in there and can see you're on Broadway.* What I think happened is that he had been tracking his wallet for the past hour. He had watched it mosey along the edge of campus and circle the roundabout with the funeral home and phallic stone powder house that the British raided in 1774. He had watched it cut in and out of side streets and stop at every pee-stained corner, blooming hydrangeas bush, rusted fire hydrant, and SLOW CHILDREN sign. *I have your wallet*, I had written to this student, unaware that I had offered him a blank well for his own projections. He had heard in that well a voice full of cryptic distortion. He had received a hostage letter.

Later that afternoon I sat in a room with no windows, a two-hundred-square-foot box illuminated only by low-hanging light bulbs, and watched my friend Takahiro Yamamoto crawl and worm his way across a dusty floor. He dragged one limb to the next limb, each movement touching the one that followed, his passage slower than that of the clouds projected on the wall behind him. Then an arm would jerk awake, a leg would shudder. He grunted and groaned and at one point humped a pillow. When he met a wall he simply kept on, creeping against the surface like ivy until he returned to the ground. He did this for four hours; I stayed for two. Shortly before I left, Taka slid past me on the floor, his elbow brushing my backpack, and muttered a sweet but unnecessary apology. He never met my eye. I had told him I was coming, but I am not sure the thought occurred to him, even as he noted my presence, that *this is my friend Simon, watching me.* He had wrapped his body inside a moment that had no articulation of itself as a "moment." Like how we never know when we are at the beginning, the end, or even the middle of things. To step outside ourselves, or even our sense of ourselves, sensing. To walk by a demolished building one late night, spot a bright white limestone under a chain-link fence, and not have to think: *Here I am, spotting a bright white limestone under a chain-link fence.*

To be nothing, in other words. To be the nothing that is something like freedom.

As far as *my* rock goes, I know what you're thinking: It is very possible my interest in it has only ever extended as far as its representations. The way Vija Celmins sets a replica cast in bronze beside its original, and the force of the two rocks, identical at first glance, creates a friction that could not be generated by the "real" rock alone. I had tried, and mostly failed, to represent that bright white limestone in the digital pages of a Word doc saved on a cloud that, if it were published, or even it were not, would be used to train a shadowy AI controlled by oligarchs to make further representations of itself. Maybe such an act of replication lights up the aura of the original. Maybe not. Here I am, telling my image of you. A rock is not a beating heart. And I am not a kind of person.

For eternity,

SIMON HAN
SOMERVILLE, MA

MERMAID STORY

by CATHERINE NIU

I'D JUST GOTTEN BACK from a tilting meeting with my boss. I had my numbers hat on. I was angry. "What's the budget, Tara? What's the cost?" Bill had shouted. We were in the midst of discussions about acquiring another bank. The idea was that two banks merged together was better than one. "All right," he'd said. He'd stomped around, eyes wild, face red, hair on end, one hand in the air. "Allrightallrightallright." I'd thought, not for the first time, that perhaps inside his furiously round paunch there was a part of my relentless mother, howling to get out.

Back at my desk, I was vaguely, intensely angry because I couldn't keep Bill's voice out. It rang up and down my back, setting off alarms. "And OI is what now?" he'd cried. "And the projected is what now?" It rang me up, ran me down, this voice, this job, question after question we sorted it out, me and Bill, Bill and me, this motherlode, this cost, god oh god. "And they're asking $$$$ for that hunk of shit? And the real valuation is closer to $? Or is it that we can only afford $?"

I'd always thought that deep down, all questions were little liars, and then Bill came along, asking them, asking them. Questions only pretended to be useful, neutral, caring, innocent, interested. Beneath them was the real dark yawn, an agitation old as time, part weapon, part human, part pain itself, eternally open, crying for help, longing to be resolved. "Say again the budget?" he'd cried, but that was not what he really wanted—no, he'd wanted the magic number that would make this bank deal swell.

I had not wanted to run the numbers during the meeting, and I did not want to run them now. There was a lot I'd wanted to say, but something—what was it?—had shut my mouth.

True, valuation was tricky. And really, in our business, the value of something was what someone was willing to pay for it. And really, someone's been willing to pay since the beginning, since maybe Eve in the Garden, so we've had time to get fancy with some formulas.

I'd told Bill that according to the comparable peers formula, $$$$ was a fair valuation of the bank. Comparable peers is one way to value something amorphous and hard to value, like a bank, or a woman, or an extraterrestrial snake. (A bank is hard to value because it makes money and also contains money, and it makes money based on how good it is at moving the money it contains. A woman is hard to value for similar reasons, but with eggs instead of money. An extraterrestrial snake is hard to value because it is extraterrestrial.) Instead of trying to project some income streams into the unknowable future, you look up the already known values of comparable peers, and you say, because it makes sense to say this, that the average value of something's peers is about the value of the thing itself. I'd named all the good big banks that were peers to this bank we were trying to buy.

"That's it," he'd said, and slammed his airborne hand flat on the conference table. "Maybe that's not the right set of comparable peers at all."

He'd been trying to get the valuation down to \$. He wouldn't say it, but that's what he was about. "Sure," I'd said. "Who's to say?"

I didn't think he was right about this, but he was my boss. My real job was a job inside my job, which was not really to offer strategic advice but to be an extra part of his brain: one part calculator, one part game for his games. "Numbers," he'd said. "Run them. For the shit peers case." He had a meeting in an hour. He would bring the new numbers to it.

So back at my desk I was angry. Up and down the backs of my thighs, the back of my heart, many things reared and rattled. I sat at my desk and fought them all off, put them all off, shoved them all off. I sat there and sat there, and then I signed myself up for a triathlon.

"Seize the body in a bright bold blend!" the drooping tea sachet beside me announced. I was angry, but it wasn't exactly anger at all. Really, I thought, if you broke things down, everything was always already part something else.

I could sign up for the Olympic distance or the Zuma distance. The Olympic distance was stated in kilometers: 1.5K swim, 40K bike, 10K run. The Zuma distance, in miles: 0.5 mi swim, 18 mi bike, 4 mi run. I wasn't an Olympian, but I could swim and bike and run. The swim was open ocean, straight down the coastline. The bike course looped twice along the Pacific Coast Highway at a gentle slope. The run course paralleled the beach, flat and fast, out to the Point Dume Cliffs and back.

In college, I used to sign myself up to run a half marathon each fall because I so dreaded my birthday that I figured a half would pull me out. After seven half marathons, I'd finally stopped signing up.

A woman's life cycled through seven-year chunks, and the twenty-eighth year was the very peak of her life—this my mother had drilled into my sisters and me like a pin to the gut. A woman would never be as beautiful, as fertile, as healthy as twenty-eight, that peak from which it was all downhill, all dying, from there on out, and now I was too far gone, I was fairly rushing toward twenty-eight now. I was a part of so much that I didn't want to be a part of—aging, calculating—so I registered for the Zuma distance triathlon.

It was February. The triathlon would be in September. My birthday would be in October. I had to meet a minimum

$350 fundraising requirement by race day to compete. I had to look myself in the face, turn twenty-eight, and accept so many things. I didn't want to ask people for money, even for a good cause (Challenged Athletes Foundation). Then I realized that Jerry, Kim, maybe all my chipper colleagues would wind up with $350 to cough up, and I couldn't ask them for money for mine. Everything had to be done—business, babies—and it had to be done now. I put off running Bill's numbers and paid the $350 myself. Then, immediately regretful, I put new numbers on his desk and got the hell out.

I lived alone in a small flat in Silver Lake. Mornings, it took thirty-five minutes, give or take, to get to the office. Evenings, closer to fifty. Nights, I was reading this book of collected poems by Dean Young. Before Dean came along, I'd stayed out drinking because I lived alone, and I was morbid, thinking. After I found Dean, I didn't stay out as long.

Dean's good big lines—they made the traffic bearable and my throat choke up. He'd be dead by late August, but just then it wasn't yet spring, and no one could know what was coming, and that old Natasha Bedingfield song had just come on the radio while some birds crossed a sky ripped with light, and I was still driving home, twenty-seven years old, singing along.

"For once I'd like to take a hammer to a diamond and just *see*," Dean would say, nights, and it never failed me, how good it was to hear even one person, just once, in all of time, say something like that.

I'd been remembering, anticipating lines like this, when suddenly ahead, in the stalled traffic, I saw the color of the old minivan painted on a strangely small truck. Red brake lights carved the hills in a slow line, like a lazing snake, and in the line, there was me, and then a couple more cars, and then the truck. We were not really moving. We were not so far apart, me and this truck. They don't make things this old color anymore.

Faintly violet plumes issued out its back. The truck bed was piled high with junk parts—old refrigerator boxes, metal bed frames, ripped chairs, ripped mattress, lumber, innumerable unnameable things, all strapped down precariously with fraying tarp and lengths of rope. There was so much time. I could've stepped out onto the stilled highway, taken my time, touched the blue truck, come back safe and sound.

When the traffic released inexplicably, as it does, the truck sped away, darting, chugging. The violet plumes streamed back from it, quickly dissolved by our collective rush. Then I was home, having my lonely dinner. Then I was reading Dean Young.

Sign up was in the spring. That summer was training season. The triathlon was in the fall.

At work, everyone was making plans to attend the Saturday training sessions, which were free, but you had to show up: 7 a.m., Malibu, open ocean swimming. To get to Malibu from Silverlake in time for 7 a.m. Saturday, you'd have to not be out sobbing and drunk in the immediate hours prior. You'd have to be sobered up on Saturday by about 5 a.m. Driving by 5:30 a.m. Parking at Zuma Beach by 6:30 a.m. Changed into your wet suit by 6:45 a.m. Running into sixty-five-degree water by 7 a.m. It was impossible.

"If you can swim, what's all the fuss?" I asked Bill, Kim, Jerry, anyone, just to hear someone say they wouldn't go train either, just to get some voices around me. Bill was too old to race like that, and Kim was carpooling with Jerry. "You should join us," she said. "We meet at Jerry's at five a.m." No one had answered my question.

We stood around the water cooler, waiting for Jerry and Bill to finish their Pop-Tarts. I was slowly filling up my thermos, remembering back in college how, after my first two half marathons, what so often happened had begun—I'd started to figure out what I could get away with, how little preparation, how much pain. After five halfs, each more painful than the last, I'd thought I ought to stop signing up, but the prospect had become frightening—five years in, the halfs had become who I was. Only after seven halfs had I worked up the nerve to stop signing up. It was horrible to realize how my mother could be right. Long ago, something had taken eternity and gutted it into seven year chunks. It had indeed taken me seven years to realize what I could give up.

I spilled some water, wiped it up. I wanted to counteract this sinking feeling I had, that I was about to orchestrate a failing.

"The fuss," Jerry said at last, swallowing, "is open ocean swimming. Very different beast. You think swimming is swimming is swimming, but that's where you're wrong. You've got the waves, the wet suit, the salt, the current, the wind, the sand, it's a lot."

I was very grateful to be answered. I pursued him with more questions. "What if you just practice extra hard with the wet suit in a pool?" I asked, and felt myself growing large, desirous, reaching. "Gargle some salt water to boot?"

"It's your race," Jerry said, retreating. "You do what you want."

That summer, I bought a wet suit. The acquisition deal was going swimmingly, and I was in a bad way. When panic crept in, I reminded myself that I knew how to swim. I didn't go to a single 7 a.m. training session for the triathlon.

Instead I was drinking too much, messy at clubs. I kept thinking maybe it wasn't so bad, maybe I'd just been this way for so long, all along, maybe I wasn't sinking so much as diving, guards down, reckless with honesty, toward my deep-down self, and getting acquainted with her, looking around.

"I've often seen you," a man would say, leaning toward me in the pulsing dark. I'd get the old thrill, the surging feeling, of some old trap splitting open and a great green rush of energy, what would happen, what could happen, now that real parts, ferocious parts, were getting involved?

In college when I was abroad, a stranger—a man I would, briefly, confusedly, love—had approached me on the cathedral steps in Milan, handsome, frowning, but in a way that did not seem angry, and this expression was what I was looking for in the clubs, what I practiced finding, what I thought I found, what I found—a man's eyes, interested, very dark—something inexplicable, a loosening in the air. An invisible, tight grid begins to move.

I'd step toward the man, into a square of light, the air parting easily around me, charming, charmed. So few things had given me pleasure, and here was something that worked. The man, looking at me, changed everything: my past, my future, seven years, seven years. His desire created a world where I was desirable—a fantasy—he gave it to me. I was no longer me; I was wanted.

Ocean light beside the beautiful man. In Milan, we walked through the galleria's glass arm of shining shops. At the far end, he pulled me into an alcove, behind some decorative trees.

"You, little girl," he said, "what are you doing to me?" One hand circled my wrist and pressed it to his hip, his belt, he was hard, his other hand on my neck. I laughed, afraid, ecstatic, I thought we'd have said things like "How are you?," go for coffee. His belt bunched up my shirt, my face in his chest—soap, cologne, metal, sweat—he wore a necklace. When a tour group approached us, we'd stood stiffly apart, like colleagues in a building. When the group left, I'd spoken again to the beautiful man to check if he could really see me. How could it be that he wanted me? He replied, touched me, this time more carefully. I didn't want that, I'd felt his retreat, I was afraid to lose the world that was only just beginning to open to me. I touched his chest, and he growled then, brief, low, a vast sound, an old sound, a giant falling over the edge of the earth.

Once, my mother parked the minivan on a gently sloped roadside parking lot, then ran out in the rain to find me. When we returned to the lot, half of the Odyssey remained in the parking spot; half jutted out into the road. The rain fell lightly. I tried to make it make sense. My mother was often angry, harried, in a rush. My mother had clusters of rain, gems of it, in her hair.

Then I saw that the Odyssey was still moving. Driverless, ever so slowly, it rolled backward down the sloped lot, further into the road, toward the far trees. I made to move, to run up behind and stop it, but my mother grabbed my arm. "Let it go," she said. She had not spoken until now.

"But—" I grasped. "There's two of us. It's right here. We can stop it." We stood so near the Odyssey, just a few feet from it, and there was so much time. Rain dripped down its blue sides, glimmered in my mother's hair.

"You don't realize," my mother said. "We would not stop it. It may be slow, but it weighs thousands of pounds."

When finally the Odyssey hit the trees, the crunch of metal, a loud crack, and the entire back windshield shattered into the seats.

Instead of training with Jerry and Kim and everyone else, I'd stay out late at the clubs. Sometimes a stranger would approach me, buy me a drink. If he seemed all right I'd be ecstatic, then brooding, especially if he was older, if he was tall. I'd breathe easier, cry just a little bit, bite his neck as he fingered me against the wall.

Plus, I didn't do nothing. I bought a bike, biked. I bought new running shoes, ran. I bought a one piece, swam in the pool. I did what I could do on my own. Then I went out into the nights, looking for what I could not.

Sure, it was sex, it was Freud, it was the little life ramming itself into the ancient facets of incomprehensible stars, but sometimes I find I'm tired of this story. That's why I think it's not all true. You don't get tired of what's really true. You don't get tired of those lines by Dean Young.

Here's what I think: Whatever's tired in a story must be at least one part wrong.

Once, cold milk leaked into the Odyssey's trunk, and even though we spent all afternoon washing and bleaching, afterward, any amount of heat would draw the milk stench out. It would float over my sisters and me as we trundled along somewhere, avoiding the ham and cheese sandwiches we'd spit up and hidden in the slotted doors, hardly breathing, yearning out the window. Sour air, crust-filled doors, where year after year we'd been fed, driven, nauseated, half asleep, the stars pounding the light of a billion years upon us, our mother chanting warnings over us, hurting us first in order to protect us. *You are not bright. You are not beautiful. You are not wise. You are not strong. You are dying. You do not have beautiful legs. You do not have beautiful eyes. You waste your precious life putting on earrings, gabbing round the house. Make money, make money, fix yourself. If you have no money, you will have nothing, you will be thrown out.* Seven years, seven years, and then a voice longer than a mother was inside us.

Even now, this coiled voice—it is so thin, so long, it is speaking.

"Go," my mother says, even now, and I step with her into the childhood bedroom furnished with pieces too grand: dark oak, dark leather. Between the dresser and the bedframe, we knock our knees against veined knobs. Again my mother stands between me and the door. "Lift your leg," she says. "One hundred times, each side. You do not have good legs. You will have to work hard."

"No," I say. I think I'd rather die than do this.

"Lift your leg," she says. Senseless words—but the expression on her face is not. Her hand cracks across my face. There is nowhere to go. She'd once been gentle, and so I am defenseless.

"Lift your leg," she says. There is something broken here

that she will fix, that I will fix, if only I will lift my leg off the ground. Something old reaches through us, beats me into the self it shows me I am.

The Odyssey did not die, shattered there in the trees, nor was it the last time we repaired it. The Odyssey died many years later, when I was twenty-one. That spring, my study abroad application came back approved. That summer, after twenty-six years together, my parents divorced. That fall, the Odyssey died while I was in Milan.

"It just stopped in the middle of Ferry Road," my sister said on the phone. "Just clicked, then went cold. They said it was a broken timing belt, so it was totaled." My father had once taught us that the timing belt was the heart of the car, which told every other piece when to move.

That fall, the corners of my mouth cracked constantly. I was exhausted. It was like a disease. It was a fog. When my vaccination report confirmed the presence of varicella in my body, which I knew ought to be there (I'd had the chicken pox as a baby), I burst into tears. That was the fog. I couldn't understand—I couldn't believe this gigantic past that I could not remember, could not see. All I could see were the years of being fed and driven, the hard crusts of punctured cheeses. But on the report was my name and proof I had lived in the world, gotten ill in a world beyond my memory.

* * *

The man I met in Milan that fall did not actually live in Milan. He was a commercial diver from Riomaggiore, and he would soon return to the coast. I took a night train to meet him in Riomaggiore, and he took me to his apartment with its windows facing the sea. He was muscled and lean. His tongue surged, a sleeve of muscle, and so did his arms, his cock, even his palms.

Sometimes he'd say things out loud like he hadn't thought them through. "So beautiful," he'd breathe, looking at me sprawled out, haggard and sunken in private nightmares. For one stunned instant I'd wonder if all along I'd mistaken myself for a minnow, when I was instead something that could sing. Then I'd think, what was beautiful here? What was he seeing that I couldn't see? My whole life—I couldn't see it?

Once among the rocks in the crashing dark, the waves fuming and the moon huge before us, he'd stood behind me, and I'd felt suddenly, violently, pressed between him and the darkness, caught there as if in the binding of some giant book. Someone somewhere was singing.

"It is a sailor's song, a legend of mermaids. A man dies swimming, following the path of moonlight out to sea," he'd said, and I'd begun to cry.

He had a fiancée, a Thai flight attendant named Li-An. Some nights, I helped him record De Andre lullabies for her. She was adjusting to a different time zone. He'd strum his old guitar and sing, his voice low, and I'd hold the phone to his lips. He'd send Li-An the recording, kiss me, enter me. They had a don't-ask-don't-tell policy.

Before I left Italy, we climbed a ruined trail, cut off years ago by landslide, to reach an abandoned café. Its large windows had long shattered on the ground. Cubes of glass crunched as we stepped through the walls.

Inside the café lay rows of bone pale cups and plates, soundless and unbroken on dark walnut shelves. Behind the counter, he flipped through a stack of postcards that were once, long ago, for sale. "For you," he'd said, handing me one that said Riomaggiore.

I don't remember taking exams that semester, but I must have. There is a transcript on file with my university, which I can still request whenever I like, for only three dollars. The transcript states exactly what courses I was enrolled in and when. It states that I passed these courses, that I graduated, that I received a specific degree. Sometimes even now, I put in a transcript request just to see if the past, pressed solid and seamed, will come back to me.

Even after Italy, men, their desire, was miraculous to me. Some outer shell rippled around the certainty of muscle underneath. On bad days, I would pull out the moments in Italy, all the times he'd been kind to me, even after I understood it wasn't only kindness, I'd pull out the moments anyway, the help they'd given me, feel their weight and shine, part truth, part lie, count it all to convince myself I wasn't impoverished.

All my life, all I'd wanted was to get away from the old colors, to be in the sea with a handsome boy, not in the sour stink, not in the trapped feeling. Summers we'd drive the eight or ten hours to the beach, the crusted doors warped with heat, and everywhere I looked—right beside me, even—there was my dream: light, shining, sexy, smelling of coconut. I'd tug off my sunhat, sweaty, pained, ungrateful, run into the sea, lay flat against the sand, wait for the burning, light filled limbs that could reach the world of beautiful men, the only world I wanted.

But soon we were back in the Odyssey. At the store, I'd watch my mother handing bills to the cashier. The cashier's gleaming nails—she'd stack and crisp the bills—the drawer clattering open with the sound of bells. She'd slide the money into a trove of money, close the drawer. She was the dragon guarding the lair, but she was also beautiful, real, right in front of me—she was a woman.

"What do you want to be when you grow up?" my mother once asked me. "Your sister wants to be a CEO." What was a CEO? I wanted to be beautiful.

"I want to be the woman who takes the money at the grocery store," I said.

"What?" my mother shouted.

Then I was afraid. "But she has all the money," I said.

"Idiot," my mother said. The Odyssey rammed down the lanes. There was nowhere to go. We were home.

I'd signed myself up for the triathlon, and then I'd seen the Odyssey, only transformed, no longer a minivan but a strangely small, freighted down, truck. Then, time hung like it does in summer, bright and endless, and then it darkened like a storm. Dean Young died. We acquired the bank. The first rounds of layoffs began. The triathlon began. Gray skies, gray seas.

"Difficult conditions this morning," the lifeguards blared. They swarmed the coastline. The water yawned and gnashed. "Strong winds."

"Get under it!" someone shouted at me. We were warming up. Again I ran into the sea. I dove down its clear green throat, only to be pounded back into the sand. I ran, dove again. Again, beat back to shore.

There was a zone of calm, a couple of inches wide, just above the sand, where the energy in the water was zero. That was where you wanted to be. That was the trick. You had to get under the big punch, get down to zero, find a way to stay down long enough.

I was trying, but my wet suit was buoyant, and I kept getting caught floating in the water, then hurled back to shore. I ran, dove again, kicked hard, dug my hand into the sand. The next wave broke over me and caught my floating legs, dragged me back by the feet. I fought the wave, pulled at the sand, came up for air.

I was still in the water. This was good. This was progress. I dove again just to practice holding on to the sand. Then I exited the water. I figured I'd gotten the gist. I had to save energy for the race itself.

Jerry slapped me on the back. "Looking good out there, Tare," he grinned. My name is Tara. He liked this joke. I stalked off. Kim waved.

Jerry loved to gloat. Jerry had gone to all twelve Malibu sessions. Jerry was going to win the triathlon.

I set up my bike. Made sure my tracker was on. Got in line on the shore. It was race time.

The warm-up had helped. Again I dove, choked down a lungful of water. I was lagging all the others, but I was getting somewhere. By the time I made it out to the first buoy, where the swim course officially began, I was in bad shape. Around me, the next heat of racers were already gathering—touching the buoy—swimming ahead. I held on to the buoy, gasping. Even here, the water rocked violently. So many of these people in the water were my colleagues.

I let go of the buoy. But I couldn't catch my breath. Each time I turned to breathe, a wave drenched me. There was nothing for it. I flipped onto my back. The water heaved up and down. I couldn't see where I was going, but I could breathe.

Gray sky, gray water, half a mile to go. I kicked hard, blindly. At several points, I remember hearing yells and lifting my head and seeing a small figure waving and hollering at me, "You're off course!" and realizing I'd been swimming out to sea.

At some point I must've been halfway down the coast, because I'd lost sight of both the beginning and the ending buoys. I lay back in the water, looked up at the sky, imagined one long line I could swim down to safety. I followed that line, body screaming. I knew then inexplicably, with a certainty I've not felt again, that I would finish the race or die trying.

When I was a child, I would go to the neighborhood swimming pool with a coin from the family cupboard and pretend I was a mermaid. It was my most unabashed game. I'd throw the coin, watch it gleam through the air, watch it plummet into the sloped, blue pool. During this game, it didn't matter who watched me, who warned me, from whatever heights, with however much authority or disdain. There in the pool's light-veined hands, the coin would lie, small and certain, a treasure within my capacities. I'd cross my ankles, take a breath, dive for the coin.

I made it to the final buoy. It took all my energy, and I clung to the buoy, afraid to let go. But time was ticking, and I had two legs left. A huge wave swept by. I realized I could use its energy. When I felt the next wave come, I let go.

The wave picked me up, like I knew it would. But it was bigger, meaner than I expected. It did not carry so much as punch me under and whirl me until I lost all sense of where the surface was. Gray water, gray sky, everything harsh and parted and yet somehow all of a piece.

I clawed out, gasped a breath, and another swell pulled me under. The wave, still swelling, was immense, magnetic. It heaved me backward, then spewed me forward, and the whole time I was trapped inside it, I was tumbling. This was it, then. How ironic to die now, here, in this leg of the race that wasn't technically any real part of the race, this treacherous stretch of nothing, from buoy to shore.

I was locked in the water, trapped, tumbling, out of air, about to breathe what I could not breathe, about to breathe despite telling myself not to breathe, because some part of the body would do it with or without me.

Then a strong hand grasped my arm and pulled me out of the water. The hand was part of a body that caught me, held me tightly, and beneath us appeared a hard and unsinkable board. Waves crashed around us, but the body and the board held me, and I did not go under, I was safe, safe now, secure in the air, above the water, no longer locked inside it. I was safe in this strength, this relief, someone more equipped than me, holding me, what rescue feels like, it was the same motion, every time.

I am more frightened now than ever by my wanting.

That evening, the small truck had darted away, then gotten stuck where the highway split in two. I'd seen the truck's predicament happening in the distance. I was coming up behind it, wondering yet again why it was carrying so much that was big and broken, what the idea was. It was garbage, all garbage, and the truck carried it strapped down carefully, like it was not.

But while before I'd been struck by the truck's predicament in terms of balance—how the tarp and rope could possibly hold all these objects in place—now the issue was speed. On both sides of the truck, cars raced past, ignoring its blinker—feebly lit, obscured by the violet plumes and the falling light—which declared that it needed to merge left. The light spluttered weakly, but you could see it, you saw it as you came up behind it, through the violet fog you knew what it was asking for, what it was trying to do. And still, no one let the truck through.

So here's what you could do. You could come up behind the truck, swing your bigger, more maneuverable car into the rushing left lane, hit the brakes. You could slow the whole line down with the fact of your body, which was, temporarily, really, a body inside a car which was also your body, just with a different kind of heart. You could throw every single part of your bodies, none of them particularly good or noble, into that relentless, rushing line. You could slow it down, just for a moment, just for kicks, or for kindness, and open a space for the truck.

"You all right?" a beautiful man shouted to me over the crashing water. I felt his strength and my own, and between us, something powerfully working. I understood that I could use it.

"Yes," I cried out to him, and so I felt his hard arms loosen, let me go. Then I stamped my feet against his thighs, pushed off from him.

When I reached the shore, I crawled out of the water. There was my bike, where I'd left it, leaning toward the mountain. I took hold of the bike, the air full of shouts, each minute running down. The sky was very bright. Up the coastline, wave after wave of bodies joined a long and shimmering line. I was still in it, this promise I'd made to myself. I remembered it. I leaned the bike, swung my leg over it. The wheels began to turn.

ADA

by JUDITH HERMANN

Translated from the German by Katy Derbyshire

I MET ADA IN the early nineties. She was the same age as me, the uncrowned queen of a far-reaching urban tribe in which most, like Ada, came from Frankfurt an der Oder on the border to Poland. This origin, according to Ada, from a city taken by storm by the Red Army at the end of the Second World War, explained why the children of that East German Frankfurt were so incapable and auto-aggressive, so excessively unstable: Frankfurt was a traumatized city, and the people born there continued to carry the trauma inside them. Ada lived out her trauma in a large, shady apartment on Helmholtzplatz in Prenzlauer Berg, which someone had occupied on her behalf in the chaotic months after the Berlin Wall came down and which couldn't be taken away from her—for a while, at least. A huge asymmetric kitchen–living room, wicker armchair with lambskin at the rear window, where Ada often sat and breastfed her baby. She was the first young mother I met, and she occupied her role with the air of a primordial mother; that wicker chair was her throne. The room full of shadows in motion, always pebbles and marbles on the long, scratched table, bouquets of branches and wild wasteland flowers in carafes, black-and-white photos pinned to the bare wall alongside Shiva with all his golden arms alongside newspaper clippings crackling in the draft. Candles and incense sticks, someone constantly tinkling away on the piano. The baby born in that room was delicate, rarely cried, big dark eyes fixed unwaveringly on the visitors who came and went, the front door unlocked. Inside the room there was no distinction made between day and night, the light always chalky as if underwater, no rules, barely a line to be crossed. It was evidently possible to be a reliable mother and to lose oneself at the same time, to give oneself up; I remember Ada at the counter of the bar we often went to at the time, I remember the dispassion with which she unbuttoned her shirt, took it off, sat before us with her upper body bared, upright and attentive; she wanted us to admire her bare breasts at two in the morning, she said they were the most beautiful out of all the breasts in the world—and we did, and we presumably assumed she was right. Where was the baby on those long nights, I think these days; at the time, I never wondered about it. Ada had a husband who amazed us by managing to study law, graduate, go about a regular job, earn money, and still be with us when we set out to climb down into the nights that descended like deep, dark wells. It was Ada who pointed out to me that the family I came from, had grown up in, didn't necessarily have to stay my family, that it was possible to leave them and look for another, a better one; she herself had cut herself loose from her Frankfurt origins and gathered a chosen family around her, made up of her husband, her child, and a close circle of other women and men. That family was good and affirming, in contrast to her biological family, whose only purpose had been to bring Ada into the world. Strangely, Ada never gave the impression while deliberating on such things that she needed any affirmation or consolation. She was invariably very composed, distanced, ironically cheerful, and possessed of a defiant aloofness; she seemed always to know something I didn't. Her deliberations on the family unsettled me; as harmless as they seem to me these days, they were amazing and important to me then. My family was a cocoon in which I was pupated, bound up and safe. Ada's views tugged a thread loose from that cocoon, pulled it apart, loosened it. It was other things that then led to its dissolution, but Ada, with the baby at her beautiful breast and her husband behind her and the others behind her husband, made the first cut.

I assume she didn't know that.

When I had my baby, five years after Ada, we began to spend the holidays together in my family's summerhouse on the North Sea. Tides and dykes, the treeless coast, the eternal triste rain were all alien to these people from Frankfurt an der Oder, Brandenburg, East Berlin. The house, once my grandmother's home, made up for that lack of familiarity. Old, decrepit, provisionally furnished with no curtains, light perforating through the windows via a tangle of climbing plants; a fantastic uncle installed in one room who took part in our nightly parties and quoted Heine, albeit rather patchily; an overgrown garden with trees for hammocks and lanterns; and friends came and went over the weeks, extended and chosen family, taking it ever more for granted. It was that house where Ada explained her family principle to me, and she did so with a gentle gesture at everything around us. Furniture, framed certificates, turn-of-the-century photographs, stopped clocks with bent hands, chipped crockery and the name of the house, which someone had hammered beneath the gable in golden letters, a hundred years ago:

Daheim: home.

All this, Ada said, is yours but it doesn't have to be. You can accept it—or let it go. You can be here but you don't have to feel responsible for anything. Anything at all. And then she stood up, walked away, and left me alone with her suggestion.

I remember a dress made of tatty indigo-blue silk that she often wore, bought for ten euros at the market on Kollwitzplatz; of all the dresses I've seen, this was the most beautiful. She took it off the only time just the two of us went out to the mud flats, as far out as possible, up to the North Sea's edge. It can't have been a coincidence that this was the one evening we spent without the others. We'd cycled to the wild beach, to the spot where the promenade ended and the dunes began. We leaned our bikes against each other, removed our shoes and walked out towards the open sea; once we reached the water, Ada took off her dress and stood naked next to me. Dusk, the sky above the land far behind us now night, the sky above the water still bright, the water mother-of-pearl, Ada's body pale and slow against the dark seam of the sea. I didn't take my dress off. She had put hers back on at some point; then we'd walked back, cycled back to the house. On another afternoon, she embraced me fiercely and unexpectedly, in the hall by the rack of rain-soaked coats, between the children's countless Wellington boots, Ada's scent suddenly so perceptible, dark, sandy, almost masculine.

In every one of those summers back then, Ada gave me flowers on my son's birthday, an August bouquet picked on the edges of the fields the night before; she was the only person who considered that tradition important. The summers were exhausting. Nerve-racking, making us happy in an exorbitant way that was painful for everyone, our goals all variable and moveable, life one long, lyrical transit. Once Ada's daughter was old enough to go to school alone in Berlin, she sometimes let her husband and child return to the city without her. One summer, her husband called me after getting back home to thank me for his stay and sum up how important it had all been for him, and then he asked me to get Ada on the phone, only to tell her that the washing machine was broken and the fridge was moldy. After that conversation, she sat down on the bench by the front door and cried. I'd never seen her cry before, and never did again. I'd like to say she left her husband shortly afterwards, met another man and had a second child; in real life, years passed between that crying on the bench and the second child, years that feel only in retrospect like a single step from one room to another. With her second child and that child's father, Ada still spent her summers at the house; we stayed close. The second child's father got the place at the head of the table; he left that spot after every meal as if he were the youngest of all the children. There was a walk on which he and Ada set out, and when they got back his glasses were broken, his shirt ripped, and his nose was bleeding. Things didn't seem to get any easier.

And yet—it's unforgettable how Ada would retire at noon with her second child, still toothless and chubby-cheeked, for a nap. How she drank a big glass of milk before the nap, the baby perched on her hip, snuggled into the curve of her arm, round cheek laid on Ada's shoulder, how she held the glass with her free right hand, downed it in one, head tipped all the way back, in deep, earnest gulps. Ritually, as if it were not milk but something far more exquisite, essential, not a drink but a color, a material she was ingesting before she escaped with her child into the in-between world of sleep, which I knew would be deep, heavy with dreams and genuinely delicious; nothing compares to a nap shared with your own child. She put the empty glass back on the table, ran the back of her hand, her wrist, over her mouth, gave me a mysterious and tender smile, went to her room and closed the door gently behind her. In the years of her separation from her first husband, the dissolution of her chosen family, her love for the father of the second child and the birth of that child, she attended analysis with Dr. Dreehüs, something I didn't know at the time; she only told me about it once the analysis, the restructuring, was over. She disbanded her family. Or her family disbanded itself. The father of her first child had a baby with a woman from Tierra del Fuego, the father of the second left Berlin. The building on Helmholtzplatz was sold and its tenants were evicted. Ada moved into a small apartment a few streets away, in a building with a camera hooked up to the doorbells, which was the beginning of the end, domesticating us all.

My child got older.

The summers were limited; sometimes school resumed in early August and we had to go back to Berlin, dog days in the city, days which always made me melancholy, full of yearning for the water, the garden, the bed in the attic room with its sandy sheets, listening to my child's breathing in the night. On one of those dog days, I was sitting in a café with Ada, and as she went to leave, she said in passing that she had to go to her analysis session, one of the last. She gestured down the street towards where the practice must be. She said: A good analyst, if you ever need one.

And that was all.

That tiny scene—the café, the remark, the gesture in that direction—crops up in my story "Dreams." Two or three sentences that deliberately conceal all else—the indigo dress, the light on the mud flats and the water, the glass of milk and the nap, the chosen families, the children, mine and hers—negating it. Those two or three sentences sum up something that's impossible to grasp. They decide in favor of a single instant, a snow-globe moment. They cast all the rest overboard.

Omission.

Writing imitates life, things disappearing, images constantly left behind, falling out of focus, sputtering out. But the autonomous decision in favor of that omission—not the glass of milk, not the dress, but yes to the café scene, although the milk and the dress are more sensual—makes it easier, balances out anguish and grief over loss and time elapsed. The father of Ada's second child once said that above all else he fell in love with her hands, her gestures; a remark I could instantly relate to. I always found Ada's hands even more beautiful than her breasts: their distinctive knuckles, slim fingernails, the explicitness with which she stretched out those hands, spread her fingers when she made her decisive, capricious observations, the elegant nonchalance with which she touched things, moved them, dropped them. She was a beautiful and quite cold woman with an upright, always rather defiant posture, although her gait might suddenly become bouncy and lighthearted.

I never trusted her; perhaps that's why it's hard for me to say I was friends with her. I'd rather say I used to know her. It would be easier to say I used to love Ada. After that occasion in the café we lost touch, I broke off contact. It may have been because I took her comment seriously, made an appointment with Dr. Dreehüs, began my analysis. Too much closeness, perhaps: Ada's sessions on the couch, my own sessions on the same couch. Dr. Dreehüs, I thought, knows something about me that I'd never tell him of my own accord, he knows things about me that Ada told him. I must have felt the need to regain control, to place the other at a safe distance. In the first years of my analysis I crashed, and I didn't want to expose myself to Ada in that state, have her observe me. We lost one another; I can't remember missing her. I was busy leaving my own family, and I didn't intend to start a new one.

—*An excerpt from* We Would Have Told Each Other Everything

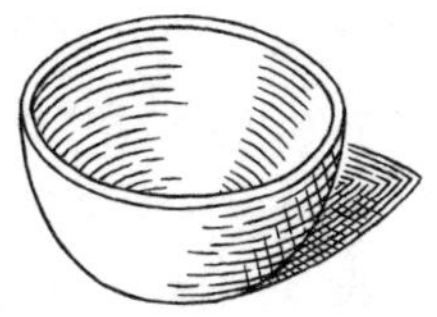

SWEET TIME

by SHRUTI SWAMY

IN THE AUGUST OF IT, of their marriage, in its long late summer, the nurse put a sad face on their door in the hospital so that the other nurses would know the baby died and they would not come in expecting a live one. It had been a boy, a little boy with a tiny, perfect little penis, who had been dead for a day inside her. He was an active child, who had kept her up with his kicking, a large child whose knees and elbows and the top of his head were always insisting against her ribs and her pelvic floor—then, day before yesterday, he had gone still. She hadn't noticed for a while—she couldn't have saved him, they told her, but still, it meant something, her failure to notice right away—then, lying on her side for a nap this strange absence suddenly descended, and she drove to the hospital talking to herself in the car: I'm just being silly!

We'll tell you this story and laugh at how frightened I was! She was not in the habit of speaking to him, which mattered to his brain development. Though it did not matter now. She was forty; her husband thirty-nine, and up for tenure: she had never been more than an adjunct all these years, in a different field. She was not the kind of woman about whom people would say oh such a shame that she never got to be a mother. Not particularly good with kids, and there was, she thought, a stiffness about her, an awkwardness that persisted, the way she held her arms at parties—that, and she was a terrible hostess, it was her husband who would always offer the guest a drink and lay a little dish of olives on the coffee table and another little dish for the pits, her husband who would horse around with the kids and carry them on his shoulders. The shame was that her husband would never be a father, people might say that about him. Thirty-nine: the door was not closed for him, he'd just need a new wife. "I don't want that!" he'd said very stricken as she lay there on the bed chatting like a child to anyone who would listen, the anesthesiologist removing the needle from her spine, the scrubbed-up doctor whose eyes were enlarged but not clarified by glasses. Actually there was silence in the room that she filled with her voice. Do you want to hold him, said the nurse: bless that nurse, bless her tears that wet the top of her mask: her own face was dry.

"No," she said, the woman who was not a mother.

"I don't want to insist," said the nurse. "But honestly, many women… they regret it if they don't. Later they regret it."

"I want to hold him," said the man who was not a father.

He was brought out in a blanket, wrapped loosely. The husband accepted it into his arms, crying and saying "oh, oh." The linguistics professor, but language had vanished, he looked like a little boy. His glasses fogged and he removed them. Oh, oh, holding the loose little hand, the hand that, in death, had lost its grasping reflex. "Vibu, do you want—"

She held out her arms. He felt much lighter than she had thought he would have felt, from how much back pain she had had. She was in the most marvelous moment of clarity, in which precisely nothing mattered. People worked their whole life for a moment like this! There was nothing in her mind at all. He had not breathed any oxygen into his lungs and so was blue, but otherwise an ingenious work of miniature: eyelashes precise against the soft cheeks, the mouth that might have spoken and sang slightly open in its silence like a dark and terrible zero. She could smell the delicate grassy edge of the amniotic fluid. "Should I—take a picture?" said the nurse.

"A picture?"

"So you," she took so many pauses, saying this all very carefully, "have something to remember him by. This is—another regret. Many women have."

SURE, WHY NOT? said the woman in what did not feel like, actually, a normal voice, when it was coming out of her mouth.

"We don't have to," said the husband.

"No, I want to."

He held out his phone to the nurse uncertainly.

"Your *phone?*" she said. "What, Victor, are you going to use this as your lockscreen?"

"Well, I don't have a camera."

"I thought you were going to bring—"

"Yes, for the birth," he said, "for the *birth*, I didn't have time—"

"Ah—if I may—you can actually hide some pictures from your library, so you don't have to see it every time you open the app," said the nurse. She accepted the phone from the husband. "Then you can just... print it out, or delete it, or whatever—you can do all that later."

"You've done this before?" asked the woman. Just their luck they'd gotten the dead-baby nurse, or maybe, the dead-baby nurse had been called, nothing to do with luck.

"Yes," said the nurse. "It's happened a few times. This kind of thing does happen."

Oh, say it, said the woman—no, she just thought it as the phone was pointed at them, and they posed, her husband draping an arm around her shoulders. She smiled, reflexively, as the flash went off, then said, "Oh god, wait, I was smiling. Take another one."

"Let me turn the flash off," her husband said.

"I can take as many as you'd like, really," said the nurse.

"You know, when bad things happen, it doesn't feel like a nightmare. It feels incredibly, amazingly real," she thought—no, she said it. The nurse was taking pictures. After a while she handed back the phone to the husband

and said, "I'll leave you folks alone now, unless you need anything. Take as long as you'd like, and you can press the call button when you're ready."

"You're so beautiful, Vibu," said the husband, openly crying. "Holding him."

"You think I'm beautiful right now?"

"I mean… I *always* think… but right now—"

"You want to hold him again?"

"It does not feel real to me," said the husband. "For the record."

"Look at your hands," she said, "and if they look right, then you're not dreaming."

"I don't want to look."

"Hey, you're living through the worst day of your life right now. Literally everything else that happens is going to be better than this."

"What is wrong with you?" he said.

"What."

"It's shock," he said to himself. Then, looking into the soft cloth in his arms, the loose weight of the unsleeping baby he said, "Looks like you. Looks exactly like you."

Then Vibhuti and Victor were at Richard and Teresa's for dinner: with Richard and Teresa, with Helen and Marta, both couples so well-meaning, so loving and whole—warm people in the beautiful house with the layered lighting scheme that Richard had bought with family money. This was not the first time she had seen her friends since the hospital: Teresa and Helen had come to visit her at her place the day after she got home, sitting in her backyard, Helen holding her hand, Teresa leaning into her shoulder with an arm around her neck. She had cried too then, moved by the sight of their tears, though not so hard that she didn't feel like she couldn't stop—it was not a performance, exactly, more like letting a small amount of pressure off, though in general she didn't understand the point of crying—not in a tough-guy way, she just didn't see the point. It's release, Helen said, but for release Vibhuti preferred laughter, or sex, both the kind that make you scream. They were looking at her now, seated at Richard and Teresa's table, with some anxiety, trying to read what tone best to strike, somber or jovial, careful or a little crazy, tender or tough, from just the scrap of her eyes over the mask.

"You can—or I mean, if you're comfortable—"

"Oh, I didn't even notice," she said, her hands going up to her face. There had been something so bare, so ordinary, about the faces of her friends—something her body had registered as shocking without fully alerting her mind. When the mask was off she could smell the food. "Where is Grace?"

"She's with her nana," said Helen.

"You could have brought her."

"I know, Vibu. I just wanted to focus on grown-up stuff tonight."

They were all sitting around the table eating olives, several glasses in.

"You didn't have to wait for us," said Victor. "We never get anywhere on time anymore—"

"We never have any place to be," she said.

"We don't mind," said Teresa. "We ate all the nice bread Marta made though, sorry."

"Assholes," Vibhuti hissed. Teresa's face wavered. "No, of course it's fine, sorry, my voice keeps being weird—"

"It's not helpful if I cry again, right?" said Teresa.

"Right," said Vibhuti.

"Oh Jesus, sit down you two," said Richard. "We're glad you're here—do you want wine?"

"Yes," they both said, chastened.

She looked at Victor. From the time they had gotten back from the hospital, she could swear that he had gotten smaller, and perhaps he had. His posture, which for many years had been upright—the result of physical therapy after a car hit him while he was crossing the street—seemed to be reverting back to the hunched-shoulder Victor of a previous life, the one he'd lived without her. The university had offered him a choice between paternity leave and bereavement leave, the former one week longer than the latter, so he had taken paternity, using his time to work through the snarls of insurance, weeding the yard bald, and drinking beers with his friend Kenneth, who Vibhuti had always thought sucked. But even she had to admit he had really shown up for Victor. Victor was back at work now—his department was of course sympathetic, but all sorts of budget cuts had calcified a bureaucratic adherence to policy. Anyway, he was up for tenure and didn't want to jeopardize it. She watched him shave carefully in the mornings, a tired jaw carved from foam. But he came alive in the classroom, he still did, his shyness dropping away, his hands growing so animated, a gentle humor emerging, the jokes akin to dad jokes but not in a painful way: she had seen him once, dropping by some paperwork on campus, through an open window, and thought, with a sick feeling in her stomach—I'm all alone here. She didn't begrudge him, she didn't blame him, he didn't blame her, they didn't fight. It's just—they didn't have words. At night, they took a sleeping pill each (she shared her prescription), wrapped their arms around each other, and listened to the breath that insisted on issuing again and again from their lungs.

Why couldn't Victor have been friends with a guy like Richard? Was it because Richard was so tall, and slightly loud, Victor more stocky and self-contained, a little more hesitant? But Kenneth was quite tall, skinny but tall with a ponytail of blond hair, and he rode his bike everywhere, even if they offered him a ride. She didn't mind the ponytail. Not the goofiness. Not the fact they always ate junk food together, like kids being bad. Well, what then? Richard always asked how you were doing and really meant it, he really wanted to know, with Kenneth, he was just waiting for you to finish talking so he could say "dope" to it and move on. They had all been friends for years and got along very well, but if Vibhuti and Teresa ever went into the other room to make drinks together, Victor always said later that he had no idea what to say to Richard, and when she said that Richard was very easy to talk to, he pointed out that *she* thought so, which was fair. She accepted her glass of wine from Richard and glanced up into his eyes as she did so—hazel—closer to green in this light; she had never noticed them before, green and brown. Teresa's were brown, but so light they were almost yellow, she had looked often into those eyes and remembered them, Helen's a brown so deep it was black, Marta's—yes, blue—she remembered as she looked, very blue and pale, like summer water. Victor with his tiger's-eye eyes—she had looked so long at those eyes she knew the irises by heart, the repeating, unrandom flecks of gold. Richard was asking him about work, and he was shrugging, saying he wasn't doing much at home anyway and couldn't complain—

"You can absolutely complain. Those fucking monsters," Helen said, she taught in the geology department.

But all this emotion embarrassed Victor, and he said that people were being kind, stepping in for him in committee work so he could just get through his classes.

Vibhuti had just quit. It was reckless, but she was too old to be adjuncting still, was paid so little it was almost like a volunteer position—as a contract worker she got only a few days of unpaid leave anyway, and she needed more, like even just for her body to recover she needed more, let alone the rest of it.

There was salad, pasta with the last of the summer squash and the summer tomatoes—Richard was the cook, and Teresa the baker. Also, broccoli, singed, the burnt parts tasted good, the whole thing smacked of lemon. There was a lull in the conversation as everyone ate, then Teresa said "the weather?" and everyone laughed, starting in on that thing they did when there was a lull, "so *hot* these days," being boring, making a joke out of it, "for this time of year"—that was Marta who did not have a naturally kind face but did something to make it kind, she narrowed her eyes as she listened to you, leaning her ear towards you instead of her eyes, and you felt your words dropping all the way in. The weather talk was migrating to climate-change gallows humor—poor Victor had come here only for her, and was not finding the company as soothing as she was, she should have left him home to watch YouTube videos about home repair—only, she had thought that human company might be good for him, the rush of human presence and human vibes. She touched his knee under the table, and he startled slightly, looked up at her, and smiled. You okay? she communicated with her eyes. I'm okay, he communicated back. She had never really been worried before, but now—well, it was illegal to fuck your students, while they were still your students, if not illegal per se, then at least frowned upon. She was not worried—not exactly—just morbidly curious—can you imagine the state of those women's wombs? That's what she thought about, their wombs and their future happy lives, when before the freshness of their adolescence upon them had made her feel only maternal and never sexually stirred.

"Sometimes I think," Marta, serious now, "I mean, I can't understand—I'm breathing this beautiful clean air and there is always as much water from this tap as I would ever want and I'm buying, like, local strawberries or whatever from the farmer's market, and I go on hikes and there are still trees—I just can't understand, you know, with my body—how many more years like this? Our lives aren't *real* anymore—"

"Of course they're real," said Teresa, "is something not real because it's going to end?"

"But when will we know when we're in the new world? When there is no more water? When there is no more fruit? When the air is ruined? How will we know? Has it already happened?"

"I don't know, it's going too fast for me," said Helen. "Ask me in a few centuries, and I can tell you."

Her son's eyes—she had opened them. Like the opposite of what you do with the dead. Gently, with her index fingers, so they could see the color, which was blue—almost a non-color, a blue gray like gunmetal. But open, he looked dead, and closed, just sleeping, so she closed them, carefully, again. The eyebrows were so faint they were practically invisible, but she could feel them under her thumbs. His eyes would have changed color, would they have been brown, like hers, or green, like Victor's? It was a kind of riddle, eyes that had never been blind, but had never seen. Was he afraid of life? Afraid of her? Had he changed his mind?

"Let's not talk about it anymore," said Teresa, looking at Vibhuti looking at Victor, and Vibhuti said:

"Oh, it's so sweet you think this is upsetting us. I love that you still think we're capable of human emotions." Then they were all looking at each other with worried looks on their faces again. “Oh, sorry, is my tone weird again?”

“Do you want to come pick some figs?” said Teresa.

“—now?”

“Yes, while we’ve still got a little light.” Vibhuti looked at Victor, who shrugged. She put her jacket on, her boots on, and it was Marta who came, not Helen, who was closer to the other women. Marta had not read the moment as an opportunity for bonding: Marta really wanted the figs and knew Helen wouldn’t get them. Her long dark hair bunched in the neck of her sweater, in the waning light, her cheeks reddened, as though slapped. But it was just that her skin was so fair it flushed at everything, heat, cold, embarrassment, and probably lust. They walked through the grass silently. It was not summer anymore, and there was not much light left, the fig tree occupied much of the darkening sky and the darkness made it feel huge, and quiet.

“Teresa, your life is so fancy—”

“Oh—no, it’s Richard—”

“I know,” said Vibhuti. “Sometimes I feel so small when I’m over here.”

“You do?” Teresa said, dismayed, and then she said, “Me too.”

Closer to the tree, the leaves and fruit were distinguishable. The fruit was black because it was ripe—the last of the sun lit the dark curves blue.

“I forgot a bowl,” said Teresa, but Vibhuti held her sweater out like a basket and said, “I don’t mind.” Blackberries had stained her shirt, some summers ago in Seattle, blackberries growing wild along the street. That had been a long summer, and she had taken her sweet time, eating as many as she could and then picking more: the fruit had been in the sun all day and was warm in her mouth. Blackberries had a more dual nature than figs, the acid in them reminded you that life was complicated and death is in everything, whereas figs, all sweet, seduced: you would never die, the figs told you, and everyone you love will be fine. She watched Teresa's fingers go delicately around the neck of the fruit.

"I miss Grace," said Vibhuti, to Marta.

"She misses you too," said Marta. "We told her about—ah—Raja."

"Did she understand?"

"Sort of. We got some picture books from the library."

Incredulously: "About stillbirth?"

"No—about death. There was one where a little boy's mom dies and he can't put his grief into words, then his grief becomes this gentle gorilla who answers all his questions about death. I actually—" she paused to accept a fig from Teresa, "we read it sometimes, just me and Helen, like, by ourselves, because it's so soothing. It doesn't pretend to know anything."

Vibhuti thought of Grace in the hospital. Grace she had held when she was only a few hours old, but it had not meant to her then what it meant to her now. Awkwardly but very gently, Marta's hand reached out to brush Vibhuti's shoulder. Vibhuti closed her eyes. She could feel the presence of the tree, a presence not dissimilar to the presence of a person on the other side of the room. Every now and then, a breeze came and lifted its leaves, whisked them against each other, making a sound like the quietest voice who nonetheless sometimes insists on speaking. Closer to the tree she could smell the fruit, and the coolness of the air, which carried the cut-grass scent over from the next-door neighbor's backyard. Figs lied about death: each fruit held the life of a tiny wasp who died frantic in fecundity and pleasure.

In another year, defying doctors' expectations, Vibhuti would hold her baby in her arms. But not *that* baby. She put her mouth to the cold fig. She pressed her teeth against it, and bit.

UNIVERSAL STUDIOS MONSTERS

WOLF-MAN!
I VANT TO SUCK
YOUR JUICY HOG!
HA HA

HOLD ON, I WANT TO FINISH THIS BOOK
WHAT ARE YOU READING?
SIGN AND SIGNIFIER
PRODUCING UN-MEANING, ASSEMBLING UN-REASON
HA HA
TOO BIG-BRAINED FOR ME. I'M JUST OUT HERE LIVING MY BEST HIMBO LIFESTYLE
DRACULA, YOU ARE A 600-YEAR-OLD, OVEREDUCATED NOBLE. YOU ARE NOT "LIVING YOUR BEST HIMBO LIFESTYLE"
SORRY
I WAS JUST BEING PLAYFUL

I KNOW HE LOVES ME, BUT I JUST GET THE IMPRESSION HE'S ALWAYS, LIKE, 20% ANNOYED AT ME
I'VE BECOME A GHOST HAUNTING MY OWN CASTLE, SKULKING AROUND BECAUSE I'M AFRAID I'M ALWAYS BUGGING HIM
I THOUGHT I'D GET LESS INSECURE AS I AGE, BUT IT'S TIPPED ALL THE WAY BACK THIS PAST CENTURY

THAT'S TOUGH
MAYBE I'M GOING THROUGH A SECOND ADOLESCENCE
I THINK MY DAD WENT THROUGH SOMETHING LIKE THAT WHEN HE MADE ME
HEY
HOW COME YOU'RE SMALLER THAN YOU LOOK IN BOOK COVERS
I SPENT THE FIRST 200 YEARS OF MY LIFE JUST LOOKING LIKE A GUY. JUST A HANDSOME GUY

THE NEXT 100
LOOKING VERY
UGLY

THEN THE NEXT
100 MOSTLY AS
A DOG

THEN I WAS A
BEAUTIFUL WOMAN
FOR 100 YEARS

AND I THOUGHT I'D
SPEND THIS 100 JUST
BEING, LIKE
LITTLE
JUST
LITTLE

I SEE. WELL, I WISH I HAD BETTER ADVICE FOR YOU
I THOUGHT SINCE YOU WERE MADE UP OF SO MANY DIFFERENT PEOPLE, YOU'D HAVE A WIDE RANGE OF EXPERIENCES TO DRAW FROM
IT'S MORE LIKE EACH BODY PART HAS A SENSE MEMORY
AND THE OLDEST PIECE OF ME IS STILL ONLY, LIKE, 37

THIS BOOK HAS A THEORY ABOUT WHY OUR MOVIES AREN'T SO IN DEMAND ANYMORE

IT SAYS HERE WE "ANIMATE THE ANXIETIES OF A BYGONE ERA," AND AS SUCH HAVE BEEN REPLACED BY MORE CONTEMPORARY--

IT'S OKAY. I DON'T NEED TO HEAR THIS

IT'S AN INTERESTING BOOK

MY FEAR IS THAT I'M BORING HIM. HE'S 600 YEARS OLD. BUT YOU--
I WAS 600 YEARS OLD ONCE, IT'S TRUE. HE'S STILL SUCH A CHILD
I KNOW HE HAS MORE LIFETIMES OF KNOWLEDGE THAN I EVER WILL
BUT THERE'S THIS CONDESCENDING EDGE TO THE WAY HE RESPONDS TO MY INTERESTS --

WE USED TO BICKER ABOUT HIS HABIT OF OVEREXPLAINING THINGS TO ME. I ASKED HIM TO LET ME LEARN ON MY OWN AND REACH MY OWN CONCLUSIONS
BUT IT'S LIKE HE RESPONDED TO THAT BY TOTALLY CHECKING OUT INSTEAD
LIKE HE OVERCORRECTED
YES!
PART OF ME WONDERS IF HE'S JUST BIDING HIS TIME UNTIL I DIE

MAYBE HE'LL SWAP ME OUT FOR SOMEONE NEW. THAT YOUNG FRANKENSTEIN
DRACULA TALKS A BIG GAME, BUT DESPITE HIS ESCAPADES, HE'S MOSTLY REMAINED MONOGAMOUS
HE'S ALMOST A LITTLE CONSERVATIVE
HE'D NEVER ADMIT IT
THANKS
THAT'S COMFORTING TO HEAR

MWA HA
HA HA HA
HA HA

DRACULA, IS THE LOCH NESS MONSTER REAL?
SORT OF

HE ONLY EXISTS SEASONALLY
ARE MERMAIDS REAL?

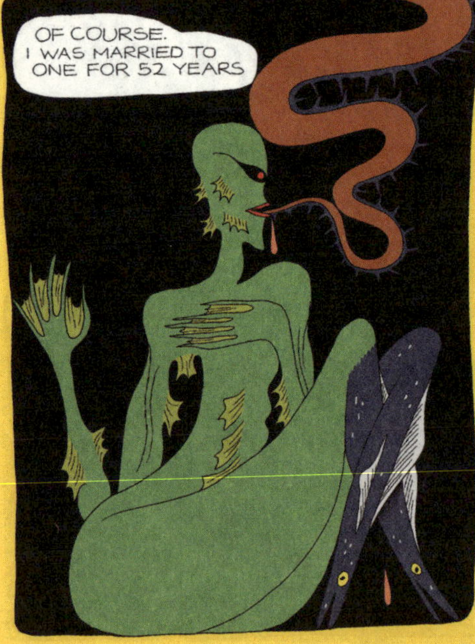
OF COURSE. I WAS MARRIED TO ONE FOR 52 YEARS

YOU WERE IN LOVE?
OBVIOUSLY

I'M STILL IN LOVE
OH...

I JUST MEAN...I'M IN LOVE WITH YOU, BUT ALSO IN LOVE WITH ALL MY FORMER LOVERS
EVEN ONES WHO DIDN'T DIE ON ME. BAD BREAK-UPS

LOVERS I ATE. LOVERS WHO TRIED TO KILL ME
I'M STILL IN LOVE WITH ALL OF THEM

I WAS AT MY LEAST DISCERNING DURING MY TIME AS A DOG

LAYING WITH HUMANS AND ANIMALS ALIKE, NEW PARTNERS EVERY NIGHT...IT BLURRED HOW I THOUGHT ABOUT "ROMANTIC" LOVE

ROMANTIC LOVE STOPPED FEELING ALL THAT DIFFERENT FROM, SAY, FRATERNAL LOVE... OR ANY OTHER KIND. I LOVED THOSE BODIES I ENCOUNTERED AT THE TIME, BUT I ALSO LOVED *HOW* I ENCOUNTERED THEM. I LOVED GETTING TO KNOW THEM

AS A DOG

THERE'S SIMULTANEOUSLY TOO MUCH TO REMEMBER AND TOO MUCH I'VE FORGOTTEN

DOES THAT MEAN YOU'RE GOING TO FORGET ME?
BABY...

I COULD NEVER FORGET THE WARMTH OF YOUR FUR AFTER YOU'VE BEEN SLEEPING IN FRONT OF THE FIREPLACE

OR THE WAY YOUR VOICE GETS HIGHER WHEN YOU READ TO ME ALOUD
TIM
QUEERING TIME,
CINEMATIC FUTU

OR THE WAY YOUR EARS PERK UP BEFORE YOU'RE FULLY ERECT

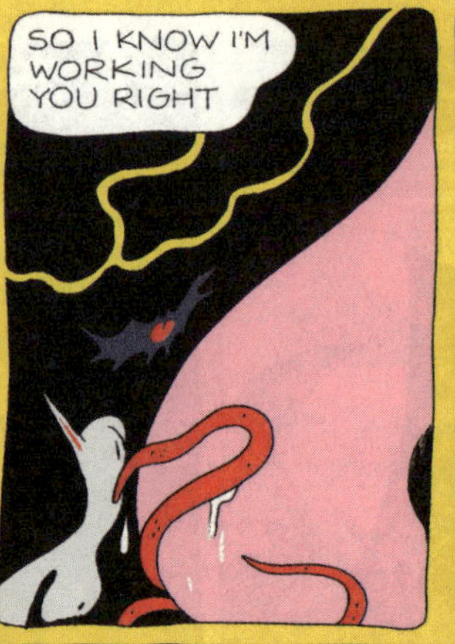
SO I KNOW I'M WORKING YOU RIGHT

OR THE DISPLACED DIRT IN THE YARD FROM WHERE YOU BURY YOUR SHIT

OR THE HOLES IN YOUR SHIRTS

OR THROWING OUT THE PENS YOU'VE CHEWED TOO MUCH ON

BUT OTHER PARTS OF YOU?

SURE, I'LL FORGET

I'LL FORGET A LITTLE

WHEN I TRANSFORMED INTO A WOLF-MAN, I LOST THE ABILITY TO RECOGNIZE MYSELF IN THE MIRROR
I RATIONALLY KNOW THE VISAGE I SEE IN THE MIRROR IS *ME*, BUT
WOLVES AREN'T A SPECIES THAT POSSESS THE ABILITY TO SELF-IDENTIFY

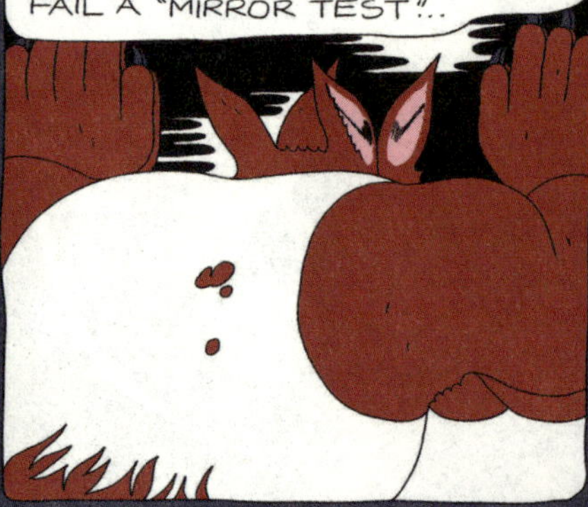

IT'S AN EXCEPTIONALISM THAT PRIVILEGES THE INDIVIDUAL ABOVE ALL

I REMEMBER WHEN DRACULA USED TO RELY ON ME TO DESCRIBE WHAT HE LOOKED LIKE

AND NOW HE RELIES ON ME

HE'LL ASK ME ABOUT EVERY DETAIL OF HIS BODY. I'LL OBLIGE

WE'LL SOMETIMES SPEND HOURS DOING THIS, THE TWO OF US LISTING OFF OUR BEASTLY ATTRIBUTES

PRESENTING

by EMILY GRAY TEDROWE

THAT WAS THE CAPTION on the photo of me that went viral at the high school where I've taught for seventeen years—that word only, nothing more. But it was enough. Whichever kid took the picture—I have my suspicions—caught me bent over a student table, chin in hand, reviewing group work on a project about imprisoned journalists in China. I was also, for some reason, balanced with one knee propped up on the seat of my rolling chair. This weirdness I own, zooming around the classroom on a chair, all teachers have their little habits, and god knows we need the energy boost. Though why I was partially kneeling on the chair, I couldn't say. However, neither the chin-in-hand nor the half-kneeling would have prompted this particular creepshot (a depressing term I'm now familiar with) were it not for the worst part: my arched back. Yes, I happened to be doing the "cow" part of cat-and-cow, a yoga stretch mandated by my physical therapist to relieve the lower-back pain that plagues me and my kind: fifty-four-year-old American men with sagging mattresses and sedentary habits.

I see you wince as you take it in, the way I happened to be mindlessly, momentarily positioned while I calculated points on an assignment. Ass cocked up, belly hanging down. My jowly face blank, mouth drooped. In front of *teenagers*.

Teenagers, with their savage humor, their blinding drive to impress, phones always in hand. All of three seconds or so, but one of them got the shot.

Oh well, you think. Embarrassing, but not much more. So the kids snickered at an awkward photo of their teacher. What's the big deal?

Ah. Let's back up a little, and I'll tell you about Whitney Young Out of Context, or @wyoutofcontext.

"So it's like *Gossip Girl*," my wife Alma said, one evening a few months ago after I told her what the day's impromptu staff meeting had been about. Detour here while she explained what *Gossip Girl* is—was—a teen melodrama about an anonymous high school blogger.

"Not really," I said, as if I wasn't just recently informed about the difference between confessional accounts (rumors, backbiting) and this kind (random photos).

There was reason for concern, according to Deanna El-Amin, one of our four vice principals and the one with a mandate least envied: student life. She didn't have to tell us, she told us, about the dangers of social media and the brutal toll paid by kids. She and Principal Hirsch were keeping a close eye on this account, and they had alerted Student Protections at Central and the Title IX folks. So far, what they'd seen was more or less innocuous—posts of sleeping students seemed to be the main theme, and no names had been used. "Still," Deanna said.

She didn't finish her thought, and she didn't need to. Every one of us in that room had experience with a student in extreme mental health crisis. Two years ago, a senior girl named Jackie Wolfe had died by suicide.

"Do we know who's running the account?" someone called from the back of the staff room.

"Working on that," Deanna said.

"It ended up being the handsome guy," Alma said, puttering in the kitchen. "On the TV show. Ava guessed it, I remember."

Ava was our daughter, now twenty and in her second year at Wisconsin. Her brother Micah graduated from Northwestern this past May, now out in Oakland after landing a good entry-level job in systems engineering.

I wished Alma would come back to the dining table. She'd cleared our plates, but I still had some beer left in my glass.

It was like this lately. She buzzed with energy and movement, whereas even the air around me felt thicker, slower.

Alma was getting ready to move out. (Not that she let me call it that.) In a few months, likely before the holidays. As soon as she and Ronnie—that is, Veronica, her best friend from childhood who recently moved to Chicago after decades in Vancouver, where they'd both grown up—found a place. No, we weren't splitting up. If we had been, at least I'd understand what was going on. Alma called it Exploring My Inner Life, this new period. She'd made a vision board, propped up on her dresser. She claimed it had nothing to do with our marriage or with me—*thanks?*—but there was this book she'd read, this one memoir, and no offense but how could I ever truly understand menopause, and how she wanted to spend time with herself, to find out what else held meaning after all those years of raising children, and how she needed to reacquaint herself with her own brain.

Reacquaint yourself with Ronnie, sounds like. The sort of thing I mumbled in that shock of it, those first conversations. Alma laughed. No, she didn't have sexual or romantic feelings for Ronnie, only the deep primal pull to be close again to someone who'd been like a sister. The coincidence of Ronnie's job (and divorce) bringing her to Chicago sparked the idea that they could find a place where Ronnie would live, and Alma would have a room to stay in. "One or two days a week," she had said. "Two or three." That's when she would be at her and Ronnie's place in some trendy neighborhood, which is where all this Inner Exploration would take place—instead of the home in Rogers Park we'd shared for twenty-three years.

She'd broken the news to me a month ago, and I hadn't handled it well. Even after she explained it would only be for a year or so—*only? or so!*—and that it had everything to do with personal growth, time for her to read and maybe write, or get out her old paints. Ronnie would barely charge her rent. I blustered. I raised my voice. I laid awake at night. Alma stayed calm, giving me time and space "to get my head around it." Our kids were no help: They thought it was a cool plan, they thought I was overreacting. "You know, Dad," Ava had said, "if she was going to, like, *divorce you*, I really don't think it would look like this."

Alma called from the kitchen. "Well, what kinds of things are they posting?"

It took a moment to make sense of her question. About the "Out of Context" account.

"Gross lunches," I said, after a moment. "Kids vaping inside their lockers."

"So, nothing too bad," Alma said. "Yet."

"Yet," I agreed.

Hey. The first I heard of the photo of my ass on @wyoutofcontext was a text from Javier, AP psych, a younger teacher I'd been friendly with over the past few years. We'd done a few dinners at each other's places, met the families. Usually sat together in staff meetings. His text read: *These fucking kids. Don't let it get to you.*

I was in my car, didn't know what he meant but didn't think too much about it. Later that night a few other vague "you okay?" messages from acquaintance-level coworkers made me feel strange and eventually led me to scroll the page.

OH MY FUCKING GOD.

"Presenting?" Alma said. She was propped up in bed, her readers on, holding my phone. "What does that mean?"

"I don't fucking know." But I had a horrible feeling it meant something sexual.

"Why were you doing that, hon?" She zoomed into the image, my tipped-up enormous ass filling the screen, and I almost fainted from humiliation. "Were you… goofing around?"

"I don't know! I was stretching my back. Or something! The point is that it's on this—Christ, this…" Our bedroom was suddenly very small and airless. I sat down. I stood up.

"There's a lot of comments," Alma said. In an amused tone that wasn't quite the outrage I'd expected.

"Jesus Christ on a stick."

"Please. It'll disappear, by tomorrow or next day."

No. No, it didn't disappear, though I literally prayed it would. Forty likes, then ninety-five likes, then four hundred something, and yes, I was checking every hour, sometimes more. Whitney Young is a big selective-enrollment school on the West Side of Chicago, storied and diverse and underfunded despite all the parent donations. Our kids were savvy as hell, pandemic-era city kids with smarts and ambition, cool and they knew it, full of ennui and joy all mixed together. In the comments they didn't say the worst things they could have. Mostly it was emojis, plenty of the peach one, also quite a few of the laugh-cry one. Javi told me how stupid it was, the whole account, and that no one paid attention. In the next breath, he'd curse out the kids for thoughtlessness and put an awkward hand on my upper arm. Give it a few pats.

I had two meetings with administrators, first Deanna and then Deanna plus Gary Freeman, one of the other vice principals. Sympathy was expressed, support was offered, and the upshot was that nothing official could be done. About the account. They were walking a fine line, Deanna said. Nobody wanted a free-speech blow-up.

"Nor do we want this," Gary said, gesturing to the phone on his desk, and then vaguely to my midsection.

"I know," I said. Burning to get out of there.

"Your name isn't on the post," Gary wanted to point out, with his tone implying how that would be worse. For me.

"I can call a special assembly," Deanna offered. "Theme it like... responsible tech use. Or an announcement in the—Oh! We could have Rickey bring it up in the newsletter! I mean not specifically *you* or that photo directly, but..."

I started shaking my head as soon as she began. No, I did not want Principal Hirsch featuring me in Hirsch's Huddle, his weekly forum in the email newsletter. Where he chided parents for double-parking at pickup, or kids for losing their gym uniforms.

"Know what my Gran said?" Gary Freeman said. "Least said, soonest mended." He pointed a pen first at me, and then at Deanna, until we both nodded agreement.

I'd taught social studies my entire career, until this year, when I added one section of global studies after Renee W. retired. The new prep was immense, and the focus on contemporary cross-cultural interaction meant chasing down contacts by phone and email during all my off-hours. The centerpiece of our European unit was supposed to involve a corresponding classroom in Lviv, Ukraine. Understandably, my co-teacher there was hard to reach. Our Zoom calls were often glitchy or rescheduled. I offered to scotch the whole thing, but Oleksandrya assured me they would make it happen. She punctuated each of her emails with a pink-cheeked smiley face.

My juniors and seniors ran the gamut from passionate and informed to checked out and amiably clueless. It had been Alma's suggestion to incorporate a creative option into each unit's final project. When I showed her a video of my student Mari performing her spoken-word piece, written from the perspective of a Uighur teen in a refugee camp, we both got chills.

Alma beamed, wiping her eyes. "See? *This* is what I want!" In living alone, she meant.

My defenses went up. "To spread awareness of Uighur Muslim genocide?"

She didn't take the bait. "To create. To become open again to the rest of the world. So much of my headspace has been"—she circled her hands at our living room, filled with photos of the kids, at our plants, at our window. "I'm sick of me, me, me, all this how am *I* doing, where am *I* falling short, what I like, what I don't like." I watched her hands, now rotating around one another, an endless cycle.

I knew what she meant. But when your wife of twenty-four years wants to get out of her own story, well… Where did that leave *our* story?

The photo of me had more likes and comments than anything else on the account. Then it became a meme on other accounts. Students reposted it with captions: *ANACONDA* and *I like big butts and I cannot lie* and *Was having a bad day then remembered I'm not this guy lololol*. I couldn't even recognize most of the usernames, and the comments underneath (*nooooo fr is this someone's actual teacher?!?*) made clear that the photo had spread beyond the school.

Either everyone was talking about it or I just felt that way. One day I came out of a bathroom stall to two students at the sinks who took one look at me, in the mirror, and then fled, wide-eyed, mouths pressed together. Shrieks of laughter ricocheted in the hallway outside. Staff members I barely knew pressed long, sympathetic eye contact on me in meetings and the parking lot. A graduate I was fond of stopped by my room, and her casual greeting made me flinch.

"How are things, Mr. Nowak?" I could barely meet her eyes.

One night just to get a break I met up with a buddy from way back, Eyal, the dad of one of Micah's first friends. He didn't know anything about my job or that photo. We got wings and a pitcher; inch by inch I relaxed. I even told him about Alma's new plan, Ronnie and the room, and so on. What I'd intended as a funny story, though, made Eyal quiet, serious.

"Tough phase," he said. "That in-between time."

I just stared.

"Don't know if you remember," Eyal went on. "But before Jen and I broke up, we were in and out of these Airbnbs, friends' guest rooms, all over the place. Honestly when the divorce came through it felt better. Cleaner, you know?" He made a chopping motion with his hand.

"Oh, it's not—I mean, we're not…" I stumbled around, trying to explain. All the while, Eyal gazed on me kindly, nodding. *I'm here for you, man.*

Alma, I could tell, believed it was better not to bring up the social media account. When I did, she put on a good act, suddenly "remembering" that a photo of my ass had gone viral at my job. Or was she just too wrapped up in all her new plans? She was seeing two and three apartments a day, FaceTiming Ronnie as she walked through empty rooms in Lakeview, the South Loop, the West Loop. They texted constantly, Alma dimming her screen so she could keep up while we watched

TV at night. A pile of stuff grew in the corner of our dining room, things she set aside to take to the new place: a set of twin bedsheets, a few pots and pans, clothes, a lot of books.

The new place. That's what she called it. Not even *my* new place! Just: the new place. An entire location I didn't factor into.

"Didn't I buy this?" I said one Saturday, holding up a coffee grinder that had been in one of her boxes, its cord neatly wrapped around the base.

"What?" Alma was in the front room, hefting one of our plants, a woebegone lemon tree, up and out of its planter for its weekly watering. She pushed back hair that had fallen forward.

"I bought this grinder." One of the kids had been with me, probably Micah. I could see us in the hardware store that used to be on Clark, the dim, crowded aisles, Micah's little hands burrowing into bins of nuts and bolts.

"That's the old one we use for spices now," Alma said, straightening up. "I thought..." She studied me. "You don't want me to take it?"

"Why this blanket?" I said, scooping up the TV room throw printed with the UW badger. A wafting smell of turmeric rose from the coffee grinder. I nudged at a few other items with the toe of my slipper. "I like this one."

"Honey." There was love in Alma's soft voice. I sensed she might come hug me, and suddenly I was so tired. I put the ragged blanket down, and set the coffee grinder on top. *Forget it.*

* * *

We are liking these presenters very much, Oleksandrya messaged me.

PRESENTERS?????!!!!! After a minute of my heart slamming around—how did she, what did she?—the lightbulb went on. My students' *presentations.* Not my "presenting." (Fucking hell, it was in my head as "my presenting"!!!)

My class had created visual documents about their families, neighborhoods, and sports or music interests, and then we posted these into the shared EduPortal where the Ukrainian students had been responding with short notes. *We are sending prayers for your safety as well.* Oleksandrya often closed her messages this way, and at first I thought it was a mirroring of my own careful expressions after the Russian invasion. Then I realized she was talking about Chicago's gun violence, the headlines that made their way to Lviv, under bombardment, half a world away.

Each day brought a few new photos posted to @wyoutofcontext: ten kids squeezed into one bathroom stall, a squashed banana in an empty sneaker, kids vaping in the back of classrooms. Once somebody posted someone else's mom's phone number, part of ongoing beef, but commenters thought this was a step too far.

Now occasionally there were shots of kids pressing their butts out, smirking over their shoulders.

"Is that—are they mimicking me?" I asked Javier, jabbing at one of them.

He pretended to need to think. "Well, not necessarily." We were in the lab, where he was cleaning up after some experiment. What I liked about Javier was that he never advised me to not check the account. Either he knew how impossible that was for me, or he could imagine that he'd be doing the same. He took on an appropriately grim facial expression every time we talked about it, which I appreciated. "But yeah," Javier sighed. "That's what they're doing."

"So many of them are boys," I said. Which surprised and bothered me. "Makes it worse," I added, thumbing furiously at my phone.

"Hang on." Javi stopped stacking plastic tubs. "Why? What do you mean?"

"Uh." I stared at him. He waited for me to get it. When I did, I was embarrassed in yet another way. It shouldn't have taken Javi—married to Adam, faculty sponsor for the LGTBQ club—to point out what was underneath what I'd said.

"Yeah, shit." I held up my hands. "I'm sorry."

He nodded, *all good.*

We hosted Ronnie for dinner a few days after she arrived in Chicago, where she'd booked a furnished apartment for a month. While she and my wife finalized their apartment search. They'd narrowed it down to a Printers Row two-bedroom with a balcony. They kept going on about that balcony.

Anyway, I did baked meatballs and the sauce, I made it as great as I always do, and Alma did her salad with all the different kinds of herbs, and it was fine, Ronnie has a dry sense of humor and refuses to take anything that seriously, and she can tell a good story. I always liked Ronnie. Ronnie was not the problem.

I didn't think? Her haircut *was* super short. I knew how dumb even noticing that was, and if she was gay now, who cared anyway. Maybe I wanted that on some level. It would be hell but a hell of a lot easier if Alma was in love with Ronnie, in that way. No one else I knew had a wife who wanted a separate place for herself in addition to her home. And who would have been fine making it public, who seemed to think there was nothing to letting other people know about this. Alma did keep it quiet, in fact, but I suspected she was doing so entirely out of respect for my feelings.

Sex. I know you're wondering about how much sex we were having, or not having, and what kind. Who really knows what people get up to, but I would guess that me and Alma had the usual stats for longtime couples. We had our little routines, our schedules. Up to then, I would have said everything was fine on both sides. But since that photo, I couldn't shake a persistent doubt. Did I still turn her on?

Had that damned image, me with my butt canted up, a primly prancing pony, wormed its way into whatever part of the brain housed the libido? If we happened to miss one of our Sunday afternooners, was that photo the reason? If she murmured, "Baby, I'm good, let me just take care of you"—was that why? Alma would never admit it, and maybe she didn't even consciously register a difference. But that didn't mean on a subliminal level she wasn't repulsed!

This was how my thoughts chased each other, around and around. From the outside, everything between us seemed normal. But sometimes an inner wave of disgust at myself would rise so fast I thought I would choke. What if that photo only confirmed to Alma that she was right to get the hell out of our bed? *Part time*, I reminded myself. Not that it helped.

I never found out who sent the photo or meme or whatever to the Ukrainian students. Nor did I pick up on the extra juicy quiet in the first part of class. The way they folded their mouths, deliberately avoided eye contact. For me, by that point, every class was brutally awkward.

I turned on the smart board and logged into EduPortal, while announcing we would need to rearrange due dates for annotated bibliographies because next week was—

Oh.

There, on my laptop—and mirrored in the six-by-eight-foot screen—was my own body, in that ass-up shape, so sad and so familiar. The photo had been posted into the chat feature we shared with the Ukrainian students, which encouraged both sets of kids to share informal updates on life: photos of themselves at home, their meals, news about celebrities they somehow all knew. You could "react" to the photos with a few emojis: thumbs up, exclamation mark, applause. Few students had been brave enough to do that on the photo of me, however. Whoever dropped the photo of me into the chat had done it at 1:23 a.m., I noticed. Also that the username was "Anonymous," a feature I hadn't known was included.

I stopped talking. All the breath in me just rushed out. I clicked the whole EduPortal closed, with a numb hand.

Before I even looked up, my students started talking. Everyone denying their own involvement through elaborate protestations: how messed up it was, they couldn't believe when they saw it, who would even… On and on.

"You know what's the worst part?" My voice, louder and hotter than I knew it should be, shut them up. "We don't get a lot of chances to interact like this, do we? With a group of peers in another country, who are going through—" I shook my head. "This is how you want to show up for them? How you want to represent our school, our…"

Amazing I could even put together sentences through the blare of emotions rushing through me, one after another: humiliation at the sight of that photo, fury at whichever little shit had done it, horror that my ass would apparently now start trending in Ukraine, anger at myself for caring, exhaustion at the whole thing, and a deep shame that our class—my class—trivialized this joint project, the one that kids and their teacher engaged in despite daily bomb shelter alerts.

That night was bad. I popped off at Alma when she tried to console me, tried to persuade me that what I'd done—yelled and ended class early—wasn't that bad. She left the room, upset, and instead of going to apologize I went out on the porch and drank another beer I didn't need.

"Knock, knock." A voice behind me. Not Alma's. "Is this the terrace of self-loathing?"

"Jesus," I said. Ronnie stepped out onto the porch. "I didn't know you were here."

"We were going to…" she said. "Well. Never mind."

"I don't need a pep talk," I said sourly. *Not from you.* Ronnie swept leaves off a chair and took a seat. She'd helped herself to a beer.

"No danger there."

Figures. What did Ronnie care about my sad sack drama? Too busy planning slumber parties with my wife.

We sat, we drank, we listened to the evening cicadas, still going strong into autumn. I had one foot up on the porch railing, and Ronnie did too, tipping her chair back.

"Did you see Zelenskyy talked to Congress? By video?" I don't know why I spoke then, or why about this.

"Yeah, I saw something about it."

"Asking for more money."

"Sure."

What a misery, I thought. The odds he was up against, the daily shattering of life in his country. All that terror. I snorted, too, to think about how Zelenskyy or any single person in Ukraine would dive at the chance to change places with me. Would rejoice at the silly little problem of humiliation because of an unflattering photo. Humiliation, what a luxury.

Ronnie brought up the US culture's weird focus on Zelenskyy's movie-star past, everyone gushing about his attractiveness and so on. We make everyone into a character, Ronnie said, and she had some other interesting observations. So we ended up having a decent conversation.

It started to get cold. "Head in?" I suggested. I could have left it at that, but of course I made some crack about how surely she and Alma had wallpaper to pick out or light fixtures to compare. Yesterday Alma told me her hand shook when she filled out the rental application, because she was so excited.

Ronnie shook her head. "Nope. That's not happening."

"What? Why?"

"Because the property managers are fuckheads, that's why." She went to open the sliding door, but I stopped her. She explained that because Alma didn't have a bank account in her own name, as opposed to the joint checking and savings we'd had for twenty-eight years— and don't get Ronnie started on her own finances, locked up in mediation with her soon-to-be ex-husband. We went in, where Alma with a fixed smile announced she had cookie dough in the oven. "Look," I said, not sure whether to apologize for earlier or for the loss of that apartment she'd loved. But Alma tapped my upper chest as she moved past me, our signal for *I know, it's okay.*

The kids in global studies were chastened and good, almost too good, for the next few weeks. They loved the unit on autumn cultural traditions: Dia de los Muertos, Samhain, Guy Fawkes, Chuseok, Diwali, and so on. They brought in food, and we played music and watched clips of harvest celebrations around the world. I messaged Oleksandrya privately to apologize for the photo, but all she sent back was another pink-cheeked smiley face. The Ukrainian kids, however, were more active in the chat than ever. For the first time they began to post photos and videos of themselves that were on the silly side. Before this they had been more serious, more orderly. Now: A boy with a giant pile of mashed potatoes on his fork pushed it all into his mouth and chewed, grinning. Girls knelt on top of each other in precarious high pyramids, cracking up when they tumbled into a pile.

Midterms arrived, and I was caught off guard by Randall, who perpetually smirked and slouched in the back of the room, and barely participated. They had been given the option of writing an essay on a topic we'd covered, or creating a slide deck on a current global issue. Most kids chose the deck, and we spent several days with the lights off, clicking through their photo-heavy presentations.

"This is, uh, about meme culture," Randall said, clutching pages. Mean culture? I asked him to repeat, and to speak up a bit.

He tugged at the hem of an oversized Supreme T-shirt. "Meme culture has been a factor of the internet since the 1900s"—he meant the 1990s, which is how kids referred to anything pre-2000—"but is now the primary way a lot of people communicate." Randall glanced up at me and back down to his paper. "One aspect of meme culture is that it's based in humor. The problem is that what is considered funny in some cultures isn't always that funny to people who may not understand the joke, or if the meme that is shared makes light of a value or a belief." By now he was reading rapidly, one word after another, no breaks, the way kids did at the front of the class.

I felt their gazes on me, warm, steady, while I watched Randall from behind my desk. I felt held by them, understood. When the class recognized some of the more famous meme images that Randall described, they laughed. This was an arena in their life, and I'd stepped inside. And it was funny, to hear him carefully break down the components of the young girl smiling at the house on fire, or Willy Wonka resting cheek on fist. He didn't mention the photo of me. Nor did he include the required secondary sources, but it was okay. When he finished and put the paper on my desk, I stood and gave him a pat on the shoulder.

What I was more concerned about, over the next few days, was my inability to be in contact with Oleksandrya. Now that the joint project's end approached—we'd agreed we'd wrap in early November—there was little she and I needed to coordinate, but her absence in the chat feature or in my email inbox made me worried. Still, in the run-up to holidays and winter break, there was so much to do I put it to the side.

Both kids came home for Thanksgiving, with their laughter, late nights, squabbles, stories, and messy rooms. Life burst back into the house, and Alma and I shared the joy. We hosted the usual feast, including Ronnie and my dad and a friend of Ava's. The food was good—I'd brined the turkey for a day and a half in an ice-salt bath in the garage—and my heart was full. Ronnie showed my dad photos on her phone from a trip to Belize. A tipsy Ava and her friend took forever to clean the kitchen, singing at the top of their lungs. Coming back from taking out a bag of trash, though, I overheard Micah asking Alma about the apartment.

"Well, I don't know," she said. Ronnie had extended her furnished month-to-month through the end of the year. Micah pressed—*what about that one you loved, with the cool windows?* I hung back in the darkened hall. Alma shook her head and changed the subject.

First thing Monday after Thanksgiving I was standing outside B&H Property Managers. Cold enough to see my breath. I'd called out, though I didn't expect this would take all day. Sure enough, when I finally got in to see this piece-of-shit broker, it didn't take more than a few minutes to say what I had to. Loud enough for their whole dump of an office to hear. Too bad for this bobo that I'd taught CPS high school for decades, because I used my full teacher voice—the one that made kids shut right up. I took my time and I laid it out for him, what he was going to do. The apartment Alma and Ronnie had wanted was gone. Nothing to do there. But this little weasel better put together a tour of the next best options, and if their completed application wasn't processed on the same goddamn day I'd raise some holy hell. To his supervisor.

When it all came together later that day, Alma cried. Ronnie pumped her fists. They showed me the place, and it was pretty great. Alma's room was small, but it was in the corner, so she got two windows.

"Two windows," she said to herself. Turning in a slow circle in the empty room.

Thursday, December 9, backstage in the school auditorium. On stage, the language teachers were finishing their medley of Christmas songs with verses taken in turn: Mandarin, French, ASL, Spanish. From the audience, students chimed in heartily. This was Whitney Young's annual holiday tradition, a teacher and staff show full of songs, skits, and school in-jokes, always capped off by "O Sole Mio" sung by Mr. Reading (sophomore math), known to be a star tenor in his church choir. In the past I'd joined the other social studies teachers for our custom version of "Twelve Days of Christmas" (*Seven sources citing, Six phones a-buzzing, FIIIIIVE MONSTER DRINKS*)—but this year I had a new role.

Just after Thanksgiving I'd grabbed Javier in the hall to explain my idea. He did a double take: You want to *what?* But then he got it. We roped in some of the younger teachers (aides, mostly), not too jaded to learn a new skit, and met during breaks to practice the choreography. Someone had sourced elf outfits, and as our song kicked in over the speakers, Javi said "Oh lord here we go" and charged out into the footlights.

The gist of the skit was a dance party in the North Pole, with the elves trying out all the new dances. *He got that swag, swag, swag* went the first song. I stayed hidden off stage while the teacher-aides and Javi did their best (worst) Running Man, Whip, Harlem Shake. The students lost it. They roared. Ms. D., a crossing guard in reindeer antlers, twerked so low to the ground that the auditorium went wild.

I gripped my prop. Was I really going to do this?

"Ready?" Javi shouted to me. His face shined with sweat.

He grabbed the mic. "Hold on, Whitney Young! We're missing someone. Yoo hoo, Santa, where are you?" Javi and all the elves mimed looking for me on stage. The kids were clapping in unison to "Ludacrismas." "Hang on, I think I see him..." The guys in the AV booth dimmed the lights. "Ladies and gentlemen, *presenting*..."

I pushed out hard with one knee on a wheeled chair, scooting onto center stage and into the spotlight. I hit my mark and paused in profile. "...Santa Claus!"

I struck the pose then, for one perfectly executed moment—stomach dropped and red-suited ass up.

The house lights went up. All the kids screamed. And if I do say so, we brought the house down.

Meme culture. Now that I was an expert, I noticed them all the time. My favorites were the Ben Affleck ones, his big face of woe, or on the beach with that magnificent, horrendous tattoo. I was riding high over winter break, after our holiday show triumph. It helped that the traffic on my own viral photo had plateaued.

One day in January I was in the car with Ava. I guess I seemed lighter about the whole thing. I shared fun facts with her that I'd learned from Randall's essay. Apparently, it was biologist Richard Dawkins who coined the meme concept: images leap from brain to brain the way genes replicate.

"Isn't that interesting?"

Ava snorted. "Spoken like a real man," she muttered from the passenger seat.

"What?"

"Dad. It's like you never heard of guys leaking their girlfriends' nudes. Or incels, or the manosphere. Or revenge porn!"

Revenge porn?! "Oh, hon, let's not—"

"It's like, I'm sorry you went through all that, with your class and stuff, but it's nothing compared to what happens to women on the internet. Every day. Literally every day."

Ava landed her point, and I subsided. I didn't want details, was scared to ask for them in fact. We continued with our errands. Once again, the sense there was so much I didn't know.

I never heard directly from Oleksandrya again. After winter break, the class wrapped its co-teaching unit and we moved on to Africa in the Post-Colonial Era. I wrote up a glowing recap of our joint project and submitted it to the EduPortal site, as required—for the continued funding of these programs—signing it on behalf of both Oleksandrya and myself. I spent a few nights searching for her on various social media platforms, but couldn't find anything definitive. Any time the news mentioned a city in Ukraine close to her area, I scrutinized the info, zooming in on Google Maps, the names of all her students scrolling through a feed inside my mind's eye.

One morning I woke to an email in my school inbox from an address I didn't recognize. I hesitated at first and almost deleted it for spam. But when I opened it, a large-file photo that took several seconds to download opened across my computer screen. It showed a group of women in military fatigues, posing together in a semicircle outside a building. Some had mouths half-open, laughing or calling out to the person taking the photo. They were all young, so young. Twenties and thirties at the most.

I could pick out Oleksandrya right away. She was second to the left, with one arm around the woman to her side, and her other hand holding a rifle. Her tucked-in smile was the one I knew from the few times we'd met over Zoom.

I magnified her hand on the rifle—four fingers curled around it, and her thumb bracing the side. Steady grip. She had nail polish on, a light purple. Maybe with sparkles, but I couldn't tell.

Last thing to say about my fifteen minutes of virtual fame. I was over at Ronnie and Alma's for dinner, something we arranged once every few weeks. It had felt awkward at first, especially those first few times I kissed my wife, left her, went to our home alone. But in time I'd grown accustomed, and it helped to see Alma's vitality, her plain old happiness. On this night, mid-March, they'd planned to serve salmon filets from a newly acquired gas grill, but with windy temps in the forties, we said fuck it and ordered ramen.

Ronnie brought me another beer—she kept them stocked with the pale ale I liked. "Wait, so it was all a hoax?"

I had just told them the news sweeping the school. Apparently, @wyoutofcontext had been taken down after a wild last post: a user who said her name was Kat claimed to have set up the entire account from her home in Sydney, Australia. She was a teenager and said she'd pretended to be one of our students on a friend's dare—Alma: "Nothing good comes from those"—and she'd chosen Whitney Young at random. Soon as she set it up, students flooded with their submissions for posts. Kat wrote that at first she thought it was funny, all the drama and rumors and vaping photos—but now her conscience told her it was time to come clean.

"So she shut it down," I said. "Just like that." Screenshots of her final post, though, had been shared all around the school. I'd heard about it from Javi, of course. He said our students were obsessed with tracking down this Kat, but no luck yet.

"Why would someone go to all that trouble?" Ronnie said. "What do you get out of that?"

I shrugged expansively, many years familiar with the unknowability of teens. My ramen had been excellent, and I lounged back in the overstuffed armchair we used to keep in the TV room.

Alma was watching me. "This is good," she said. "For you."

"Yep." All gone forever: that dumb photo, all those comments, likes, emojis. Vanished back into the hormonal ether from where it came. Even though I'd managed to delete the app from my phone, any glimpse of its icon or brand colors could still make me shudder. "That's that, I guess. None of it really had to do with me. With the school, I mean."

Now that the account was down, I felt like I could breathe again. Australia was about as far away as you could get, and how could I really care what teens from down under had thought about my stupid pose? Surely, they had their own old guys to laugh at.

"Huh," Ronnie said.

"What?"

"Well, no reason to believe this Kat's story, is there? I mean, couldn't that also be a hoax?"

"No." The idea unsettled me. "I mean, I don't know."

"Anyone can make up whatever they want. First claiming it's real, then saying it's not."

"Yes, I know how the internet works, Ronnie." What would that mean, though? That someone—another student, here or in Australia or anywhere in between, could resurrect the account and maybe even my photo? Start it all over again? A gritty little seed of agitation stuck in my brain.

"It doesn't matter," Alma said. "The point is that it's over." She reached over and took my hand. Her fingers were as soft as ever.

"Sure," Ronnie said.

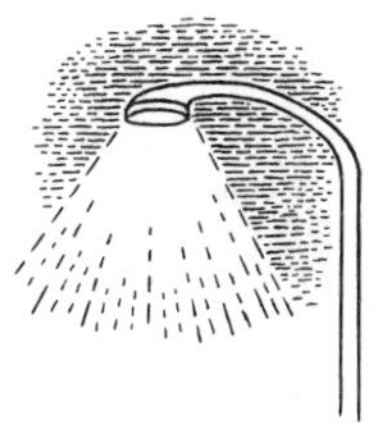

PART TIME JOB

by SAM MUNSON

VICTOR H GOT FIRED on a Monday.

His boss said: it's not your fault, the company is having a bad year. In fact, you're pretty good at your job.

Luckily Victor H had some money saved up. Not a fortune, but enough to get by for a while. As long as he got a part-time job. He had not had a job like that since he was a kid, and frankly, the prospect of getting another such job made him feel happy and free.

He looked on the internet for part-time jobs, and there were a few. He emailed and called the people who posted them. One was for a receptionist job, another a "data manager." The job posters all seemed friendly. But once they saw Victor H's résumé, they all said the same thing. He was overqualified, they didn't think the work would be engaging enough for him. Even when he applied to cashier jobs in grocery stores and coffee shops, he was told he was overqualified.

The obvious answer was to go to work for one of the delivery services. But he soon realized that the delivery job presented him with a real problem. The money he made was not enough to get by long term, and the job also consumed enough of his time that it made the search for a more sustainable position impossible.

He did not give up. That would have been stupid. But every day he began to feel more and more worried about what he was going to do.

One night, he delivered a meal to a customer whose name he thought he recognized. And when the man opened the door, Victor H saw it was the same guy: his old friend from elementary school, Prosper M.

Prosper M recognized him right away.

Prosper M said: how's it going, man?

Victor H saw Prosper M's apartment. It was huge. The windows looked out over the river. Big leather couches formed an oblong in the living room. A fire was burning in the fireplace. Victor H smelled its sweet smell.

Prosper M said: come in, we should have a drink and catch up.

Victor H felt ashamed. He was going to have to admit to this rich guy how close to broke he was. But then he thought: fuck it, that's nothing to be ashamed of. Besides, Prosper M had grown up in a family so poor they had trouble affording food. Victor H used to give him half his lunches when he was a boy. So he went inside.

They had a few drinks, and Prosper H brought out food: smoked fish, real caviar. Plus a large bottle of vodka, a brand Victor H had never even heard of. Eventually, the conversation took a turn Victor H had feared.

Prosper M said: so you work in delivery, huh?

Victor H said: yes, absolutely—a great way to make money, but I'm trying to figure out my next thing.

Prosper M said: yeah, I know, I work in delivery too.

Victor H thought this was a joke. That Prosper M meant he worked for a logistics firm or a shipping company. And he waited for the next phase of the joke. But Prosper M was smiling a friendly, frank smile.

Victor H said: what do you mean? How do you afford all this?

Prosper M said: where I work pays well. And it's not drugs, a lot of people think that. You interested? If you want me to set you up, it's no problem.

Victor H said: can you tell me more about it?

Prosper M said: not until you get signed up. But it's not drugs or prostitutes, don't worry.

It turned out signing up was easy. All Victor H had to do was give Prosper M his mailing address. Victor H hung out for another few hours, getting drunker and drunker. He was pleased to discover that Prosper M was just the same as he had been when he was a kid: happy-go-lucky, not stuck-up, and friendly.

Victor H had a terrible hangover the next day, but he didn't let it stop him from working. He did five deliveries that afternoon and another ten before midnight. He was exhausted when he got back to his apartment. But he saw a package in his mailbox and took it with him to open.

There was a return address: COMPREHENSIVE SOLUTION ENGINEERING, with a PO box. No phone number or anything like that. When he opened the cardboard, he found some bubble wrap taped around a small, heavy black object. It was an old-fashioned flip cell phone with a matte case and a short, thick antenna. A charging cord was taped to the phone's back. He plugged it in and watched until the little red light next to the cord socket turned green. Then he turned the phone on.

Nothing happened. He left the phone in the kitchen while he checked his other phone for any jobs available the next day. Then he lay down on his sofa, just to rest. He closed his eyes.

A shrill noise woke him up. He knew it was the phone. It was the one unfamiliar sound.

When he answered it, he heard a gruff voice.

The voice said: is this Victor H?

Victor H said: yes.

The voice said: go to the corner of Roosevelt and One Hundred Fourteenth Street. Half an hour.

Then, nothing. Victor H drank the cold leftover coffee in the pot and headed out. He got to the corner in plenty of time. It was dark, no other pedestrians. Despite the late hour, cars filled the lot. He heard music in the distance: they must be having a concert at the stadium. He worried at first this was a scam. He'd been sent here to get robbed. Then he started laughing at the idea that Prosper M would trick him into getting robbed. Like he was so desperate he was robbing a broke man.

It was only after his head had cleared completely that Victor H realized he had no idea what he was picking up. He assumed someone would arrive and explain everything. But it was almost the appointed time, and he still had not seen anybody.

The phone rang again, right as the half hour elapsed. When he answered, it was the same voice.

The voice said: you see that concrete chunk?

Victor H did see a concrete chunk. It was lying on the sidewalk at the foot of the train track stanchion, and it had clearly been broken away from the curb.

The voice said: pick it up and, without looking, throw it backward over your head. Over the fence and into the parking lot.

Victor said: what?

The voice said: you heard me. Pick up the concrete chunk and, without looking, throw it backward over your head. Over the fence and into the parking lot.

Victor was silent for a while.

The voice said: hello? You there?

Victor said: is this a joke?

The voice said: look, this a five-grand gig. You don't want it, I'll call the next guy.

Victor said: no, no.

Five thousand dollars was almost his entire previous monthly salary.

Victor H said: can I put the phone down while I throw it?

The voice said: whatever works.

Victor set the phone in the thin strip of high weeds next to the lot fence and grabbed the chunk. Then he readied himself. The chunk was heavy but manageable. He gave a few practice swings, tensed up, and threw the chunk back over his head.

He turned around right away and watched it sail through the air. He had thrown it hard and farther, in a higher, truer arc, than he would have guessed he could. It landed right on the windshield of a car in the lot near the fence and smashed it in. The inside dome light came on and an alarm started howling. There was, he saw, a raggedy white stuffed toy dog in the back seat. He ran off, on instinct. Then he remembered: the phone. He dashed back and grabbed it and started to run again, before he decided that running made him look guilty and a brisk walk was better.

The voice said (from a distance; Victor H was holding the phone by his waist): hello? Hello?

Victor H said: I'm here.

The voice said: good work. You'll get paid tomorrow. Have a good night.

Then they hung up. The alarm was still howling. A car started to slow. Victor kept walking. His heart felt like it was expanding, his lungs, his eyes. His testicles throbbed, and the soles of his feet. He felt close to vomiting the whole way home on the train, and he stared out the window at every stop, down onto the avenue, looking for the lights of police cars.

No police cars came. He got back to his building and found his exhaustion had disappeared. Victor H stayed awake almost until dawn. Leaning out of his thrown-open window and inhaling the cold, scentless air of the night.

The money arrived just as the voice on the phone said it would.

Shortly after Victor H awoke—he had slept much later than usual—someone buzzed his intercom. He pressed the button to speak, but no one answered. He trotted down the stairs and found a brown, stiffish envelope in his mailbox. It contained five thousand dollars, in twenties and hundreds. The bills new and pale.

He counted them again and again in his kitchen. At first he thought he should deposit them in his checking account. But then he decided to keep them in ready cash.

After all, this way, no one official knew about the money. Ergo, it did not exist. Even though he had done nothing wrong to earn it. A windshield: what's that? And yes, he had to admit it was strange. To be paid for an action like that. He tried to think of a reason for it. The only one that came to mind was: the car owner had owed a debt to some criminal. But Victor H knew that was bullshit. The voice had not told him to aim at a specific car. Quite the opposite. Then there was the question of how they had observed him. He assumed they must have used a drone, or a camera with great resolution placed in a building near the corner. Yet he had not seen or heard a drone (though maybe it had been too far up for that) and there were no buildings along the stretch of the avenue. Just the train and parking lots north and south.

Still, he had the money. The sum itself was more than

enough to set his mind at ease about the immediate future. So when Prosper M texted him that day to ask if everything was all right, Victor H wrote back that everything had gone fine. Prosper M then invited him to a party at his apartment that evening, and Victor H wrote that he'd come.

The party was a lot of fun. Victor H had been worried he would be miserable, because he didn't know anyone other than the host. But Prosper M's friends all had the same temperament: relaxed, happy, and easygoing. They welcomed Victor H, chatted with him, and he found out that they all—with the exception of Prosper M's younger sister, whom Victor H remembered as a silent, chubby child—worked in deliveries, for the same company as Prosper M. They congratulated Victor H on having signed up. It was a lot of fun and an easy way to make money.

About this Victor H felt awkward. Sure, it was easy, and it had been exciting. But was it fun?

There had been a toy in the back of the car he smashed, which meant the owner probably had a family. At least Victor H did not have to worry about kids. Who knows what kind of economic problems he had caused by fucking up a family man's car. And the kid would be scared and upset as well.

On the other hand, he had to think of himself first. And to a certain extent all these worries were inflated, a shitty sentimentalism. He had kept the money, after all. He had used it to buy the champagne he had brought with him.

The other partygoers did not ask him about his gig; what he had done for it. They did not discuss it with each other in specific terms.

One, a towering woman with a near-shaven head, said: yeah, I had to go all the way out to Staten Island!

Prosper M said: I hope you got extra for that.

And all the partygoers laughed, the towering woman hardest of all. A few others made vague, subsequent references after this. Victor H added his own, that he had been "called out"' to Shea Stadium.

The towering woman said: your first time? That's barbaric!

Again everyone laughed. The towering woman glanced at Victor H until he started laughing as well.

Victor H got drunk quickly, because he had forgotten to eat dinner. The more he drank the harder it was for him to keep his mouth shut about the delivery. But he managed, he kept up with the talk somehow. The other partygoers did not return to the subject much. Instead they talked about movies they had seen or concerts they had gone to. They also discussed meals, their apartments, and vacations they planned to take. Above all, they discussed books. Novels, primarily. Essay collections after that. And they even, to Victor H's surprise, discussed reviews of these books.

Here Victor H felt a little less uneasy. He did not read much, but what he did read he felt able to talk about, and when he added his comments no one sneered or dismissed them. Apparently, the partygoers even had a monthly "book club" where they all met at Prosper M's house to discuss what they were reading.

The towering woman said: you should come to the next one.

Prosper M said: yeah, man, for sure.

Victor H said: I'd love to, sounds great.

Throughout all of this, Prosper M's sister remained silent. She had a glass of vodka in her hand. Glaucous condensation covered the glass. At times she raised it to her mouth and let some vodka dribble past her lips. Victor H did not want to make her any more uncomfortable. It was clear she was not enjoying herself. But he found that his eyes strayed to her again and again, simply because she looked so sad.

Victor H went out on the balcony to smoke a cigarette. The towering woman was with him. When they came back inside, Prosper M's sister was gone.

The party went on until after two. Victor was very drunk. It ended only because all the partygoers began getting calls on their delivery phones. First, the towering woman. When her phone rang, she stopped laughing in the middle of a laugh and answered it. Then, without saying goodbye, she walked rapidly to the coat closet in the vestibule, grabbed her jacket, and left. The other soon followed: their phones all rang one after another.

Victor's did too.

The voice said: go to the East River Esplanade. Near Ninety-First Street. Forty-five minutes.

Victor H had plenty of time, so he stopped to take a piss first. When he was done, he heard a sound through the bathroom door that he recognized through his drunkenness. The sound of someone sobbing. It was soft and quiet, but it was clear.

He walked back through the semi-dark hall until the sound got louder. There, through a doorway that opened up into a room with a couch and a big TV, he saw Prosper M's sister.

She was sitting on the couch, weeping with her round face in her hands. Her body rocking lightly. Victor H felt uneasy. Should he say something? Perhaps she needed help. Yet it was not his business, he decided, and hurried back out front, to say goodbye to Prosper M and get to the destination.

That part of the esplanade was empty. A white streetlight cast a hard glow on the hexagonal pavement stones. The river rose and fell, a little greasy. The white foam strung along the swell blazed where the streetlamp light touched it.

This time, Victor H had to wait a little longer for the phone to ring again. His drunkenness increased, even though he had drunk almost a gallon bottle of water that he'd bought on the way. When the phone rang, the sound was so loud it startled him. It startled an old man who had been, Victor H now saw, sleeping on a bench under a gray quilt just outside the circle of lamplight. He sat up as Victor H listened.

The voice said: you see that old man?

Victor H hesitated again.

The voice said: christ, this is the second time. You want the job or not? This is a ten-thousand-dollar job. You'll be paid tomorrow.

Victor H said: yes, yes, I see him.

The voice said: go walk up to him.

Victor H felt dizzy. His legs were weak and wavery. But he forced himself to approach the old man, who was sitting upright now but dozing.

The voice said: is the old man asleep or awake?

Victor H said: fuck, I can't tell.

The voice said: well, wake him up. He needs to be awake for this.

Victor H bent down and tried to wake the old man up. The old man stank, like piss and shit. He was barefoot. The skin on his feet was chapped. Huge horns and ridges of flesh had accreted on the toe tips and his heels. Dirt had gathered in the cracks of the skin. On one ankle a deep, circular wound was open. Its edges purple and black and its center raw red. He shook the old man's shoulder until he opened his eyes. The irises were piss yellow.

The voice said: he awake?

Victor H said: yes, he's awake.

The voice said: give him the phone. Tell him to listen. But make sure you get it back or you won't get paid.

Victor H handed the old man the phone.

Victor H said: hey, someone wants to talk to you.

The old man took the phone. Like he had been expecting a call. He flapped his lips twice, and his raw gums gleamed. Victor H couldn't hear what the voice said to him. But before he knew what was happening, the old man had gotten up with the phone and started to run north, along the esplanade.

Victor H was so startled he lagged for a second. The old man was moving much faster than he would have thought.

Victor H yelled: hey, come back! Give it back!

The old man looked over his shoulder. He was passing through the cone of light another streetlamp cast. The light fell on his collapsed face. He looked frightened, his tongue was edging around his mouth and his gums gleamed again.

He started to run even faster, though he was also hobbling a little. It did not take long for Victor H to catch up with him and head him off.

Victor H said: hey, give it back, I need it.

The old man looked at him with his yellowed eyes and tried to dodge past. Victor H blocked him. The old man shoved him, and Victor H stumbled. The stench helped the old man, it hampered Victor H's breathing. Now the old man was running again, heading west toward the more populated streets. If he got there, no way Victor could get the phone without the old man making a huge scene. And he did not want to involve the police. He knew the voice on the phone would be annoyed by that. So he ran as fast as he could until he was right behind the old man. Then he took a deep breath and held it and launched himself through the air.

He hit the old man with the full weight of his body. The old man collapsed at once. He lay underneath Victor H. The stench was stronger than before. Almost choking. Victor H grabbed the phone out from under the man and jumped up. He was close to vomiting as he trotted west.

He kept looking behind him to see if the old man was getting up. He had not risen by the time Victor H reached the avenue. And then it was too dark to see.

The payment arrived the next day. The same brown envelope, the same pale bills. The same fresh acidic smell from the clean money. Victor H counted it and counted it. It was more than he had ever earned at one time before. He kept it by him on his desk as he read the news. He did not find any reports of deaths, which made him feel a little better. Though there was no guarantee that the old man, if he had died, had been discovered yet. Or if he had died and been found, that did not mean it would be considered news. For all anyone knew, the old fucker might have died of a heart attack. Again: why this old man, of all the old men in the city? Well, it was possible he, too, owed a debt. Yes, debts often lead to becoming a beggar. Though if the old man really was a vagrant, how could they have spotted him, unless they had some way of following him around? And that, if it existed, would have cost enough to really cut into the value of the recovered debt. Which, it should be noted, seemed unlikely to have been recovered. Still, a collection effort was—Victor H decided—the only possible reason. Nothing else made any sense.

He decided to buy a new suit. He had needed one for months, and now he finally had enough money and enough time to really pick a good one. He spent almost an hour walking up and down the avenue in front of expensive mens' stores. In front of each one stood a security guard, smiling warily. At last he worked up enough courage to go in. The store worker, a young woman in a green velvet blazer, smiled too. Her teeth blazing.

The store worker said: how can we help you?

Victor H said: I am looking for a suit.

The store worker said: tell me a bit more about what you had in mind.

Victor H, to his total surprise, discovered that he could not in fact supply any details about the suit. About its color or cut. About its material. The idea, *suit*, had loomed up as the store worker spoke, but it lacked its particulars. Just a grayish, ashen hole. The store worker was staring at him. Her smile was hardening.

The store worker said: sir, could you tell me a bit more? It's hard for us to help you if you don't. Or I could show you some different cuts and different materials. Would that work?

Victor H said: no, no, I know I need a suit, just hang on.

He found that his mouth was getting dryer and dryer and that his throat felt like it was closing up. The store worker nodded, but not at him. In one of the fitting mirrors, Victor H saw the security guard walk in and move toward him.

Victor H said: why are you calling security? I haven't done anything wrong.

The store worker said: sir, we think you might be more comfortable shopping elsewhere.

Victor H said: that's unfair, I have just as much right as anyone else.

His voice was loud and frayed. It made the other customers look around, as well as the thin, greasy-faced man behind the counter. The security guard was getting closer. He had his hands spread apart lightly. Like he was trying to grab a fish. Victor H darted out past him—stone bald, pinkish—before he could say anything.

Back at his apartment, Victor H counted the second payment again. It was still all there. With the mostly unspent first payment and his other savings, he calculated, this cash would be enough for him to get by for a long while. So if he did not want to take any more jobs, he did not have to. No: he simply did not have to. It was his choice. The phone had no control over him. In fact, he decided he was going to get rid of it. To resign from the service. His first thought was to call back. But the phone did not display the number of the most recent call, and he had no idea what it was. He texted Prosper M to ask, on his normal phone. But Prosper M did not respond, even though he read the text. Victor H decided that he did not need Prosper M's advice. He would simply get rid of the phone himself, and then he'd be free of the problem forever. He was about to toss it into the kitchen garbage can when it started ringing.

Victor H felt relieved. He could just tell the guy himself. He answered and was already starting to speak when the voice interrupted him.

The voice said: you're in the kitchen, right?

Victor H felt suddenly sick.

The voice said: we have a fifty-thousand-dollar job on deck. You interested?

Still Victor H felt too sick to speak.

The voice said: you don't even have to go anywhere? See the knife—the big one in the chef's block?

Victor H did have a chef's block on the countertop: cheap pinewood, with five dented knives in the slots. The biggest one was the only one he really used. He was getting ready to throw the phone away once more when the voice started speaking again.

The voice said: no, don't throw the phone away. Then we have to levy penalties. The phone's not yours. You understand that.

Victor H said: so how do I return it?

The voice said: don't be so hasty. You haven't even heard what the job is yet.

Victor H said: I just want to return the phone.

The voice said: actually, the rate went up. It's now a hundred-thousand-dollar job. Those are rare. Not even your friend has had one of those.

Victor H did not say anything.

The voice went on.

The voice said: you see that knife there? The big one?

Victor H said: yes, I see it.

The voice said: take it out of the chef's block.

Victor H said: then what?

The voice said: if you want the money, you must follow the procedure. Take the knife out, and then you'll know.

That same effervescent illness was coursing through his legs, his knees shaking. He had his hand on the knife handle. The blade came out of the chef's block with its usual slightly rusty, soft cry.

The voice said: get one of those cucumbers out of your fridge. Cut two slices and take a nap with them on your eyes. Like in the face-cream advertisements.

Then the line went dead. Victor H found the knife was shaking in his hand. He had purchased the cucumbers that morning on his way back from the suit shop. It was hard, at first, for him to fall asleep with the slices on his eyes. They were wet and uncomfortable, a little too cold. But after a while, they warmed a bit and he began to feel sleepy. He had been awake too late the night before, drunk too much.

Sleep came before he realized it. When he woke up, it was eleven o'clock in the morning. One of the cucumber slices had fallen off his eyes. He threw it and the other one away. His intercom buzzed. He crept downstairs and found a brown cardboard box with his name and address on it.

He carried it upstairs and opened it. His hands shook. Inside he found a thousand hundred-dollar bills. Clean and pale, giving off their sour new smell.

That afternoon, Victor H took the phone to the esplanade and threw it over the low fence into the river. He threw it hard enough to get it clear of the concrete blocks at the waterline, and he watched it sink. As it flew through the air, it started to ring. But the water silenced the tinny sound.

At home, he threw out the knife he had used to cut up the cucumber. He threw out the rest of his knives as well. All the tools in his toolbox, his boxes of nails and screws, the large rolls of copper wire and twine he had obtained and forgotten about, and all the chemical cleansers under his sink. He got rid of the laundry bleach and detergent he kept in the back of the clothes closet. He threw out his razor and the blades: he used an old-fashioned kind, with thin sharp blades you had to place between the two metal plates of the head. He emptied the medicine cabinet. Aspirin, sleeping pills, the expired painkillers left over from his root canal last year.

When he had gathered all this up in a black garbage bag, he hesitated. After all, he had gotten rid of the phone… nonetheless, he took the bag down to the trash room and stuffed it into the compactor chute.

To be honest, all his worries seemed absurd. First of all, he was guilty of—what? Breaking a car windshield. Not much of a crime. Even if they could prove it was him, which no one could. Then there was the old man. But, of course, nothing had happened there either. The old man had stolen his phone. Not even *his* phone, but a phone given to him that nonetheless belonged to some commercial organization. And if anything bad had happened, then it would have shown up in the news. The news recorded almost every crime, especially when the victims were helpless. Since no mention had appeared, the old bastard was fine. Even if he wasn't, so what? The world did not need any more filthy, sleeping bums. Besides, no one ever died or even got really hurt just from being tackled and knocked down. There was no way the old man could have survived his life as a vagrant for so long if he was that weak. As for the phone itself, it was in the river. The voice on the other end had no way of contacting Victor H, except through the mail. And what could he do? Send a threatening letter demanding the return of his property? Let's say the voice hired some lawyers and claimed the phone was worth the whole hundred thousand. Even then, Victor H could simply give the money back and be whole. If he moved, however, the voice would not be able to find him. So that was clearly what must happen.

The search for a new place was easier than he had imagined. He had never lived in a small town before, and there were a lot of them nearby, with lots of cheap, nice houses for rent. He found one place that was so cheap his current cash would last him for almost three years. And if he could not find some new job before then, he deserved to starve.

The owner of the house answered her email quickly. She was a lady about the same age as Victor H's mother. The place was in great shape. Apparently the reason she needed a tenant was mostly to have someone there to look after the place. Not that Victor H would have to be a handyman. No, just to make sure there were no leaks or fires, no burglaries.

She spent most of her time in California, but she was going to be at the rental house that week. Victor H arranged a day to go see her. The town was on the commuter rail line, and the house itself was only a few minutes' walk from the station.

While he was boarding the train, Victor H thought he saw someone he knew. Just a quick glimpse in his peripheral vision. A woman. With a round face, possibly. Whoever it was, he only saw her for a moment, and he attributed the resemblance to his overexcited nerves. Besides, he did not see anyone when he walked the length of the train, and did not see anyone once he got off at his stop. He stayed on the platform for ten minutes—he had luckily arrived early—and looked all around, trotted to one end and then back to the other, and checked inside the white-painted station house. No one there. And both bathrooms were locked.

The air was clear and cool, sweet smelling. The town was quiet. A few cars passed him on the main street. There were people in the coffee shop he passed, young and old. A kid rode by on a red bike. The bike had a basket attached to the front, and the basket was filled with newspapers. He followed the main street until the commercial buildings ended and then turned north. The walk to the house took him out of the town proper and into the mild hills behind it. The path was quiet, a footpath to one side of a country road in decent repair. He did not see a single car as he walked, and he checked behind him and around him to see if he was being followed.

The house itself looked exactly as it had in the photographs: small, whitish, with some slightly leprous bricks peeping through the paint, black shutters, and a wet-looking elm tree hanging over the roof. The air smelled even sweeter here, like the sweet, rotten smell that comes from wet leaves. Victor H found the smell relaxing. He knocked on the door and waited. A bird was chirping, a liquid, sawing noise. The owner answered and invited him in. She had silver hair and a large mole on her right cheek.

The owner was very straightforward. She said Victor seemed responsible, and she liked the fact that he could pay the three months' rent in cash in advance. The place was ready to move into right away. All that remained was to sign the papers. The property owner had them ready, and Victor H signed with pleasure.

The owner said: great, you can move in whenever you're ready. Just let me know, and I will clear out of here beforehand.

She handed Victor H the keys. Three of them—front door, back door, basement door—on a flimsy, hairlike metal ring.

The owner said: we should celebrate! I have some wine, or I can make coffee.

Victor H said: coffee would be great.

The owner went to the kitchen, which was in the rear of the house. Victor H waited in the living room. The window was open and the sweet, cool air floated in. Victor H closed his eyes and let the draft roll over him. It was just strong enough to move his hair.

A crisp, deafening boom followed by deep, shrill cry broke his reverie. Then a noise like coughing. Victor H ran back to the kitchen. He worried the owner had fallen or had a heart attack. She was the right age for it.

The owner was bent at the waist over the small table in the dining room. There was a round, ragged hole in the back of her white shirt and a red spray, irregular and ovoid, on the wall behind her. The coughing noise came from her. Blood pooled on the tabletop under her working mouth. Standing opposite her and holding a pistol was Prosper M's sister. She held the pistol in her right hand. She saw Victor H and aimed the gun right at him. She had an old-fashioned flip phone in her left hand, he saw. Right next to her sunlit ear.

Prosper M's sister said (into the phone): yes, yes, I'm still here.

She was pointing the gun right at Victor H. Behind her the light back door swung open and shut in the breeze.

Proper M's sister said: no, no, don't hang up. I want the job. I definitely want the job. Hang on.

She fell silent for a moment. Her cheeks were wet and shiny and her eyes a little red.

Prosper M's sister held the phone toward Victor H. She wagged the gun. Deep shadow in the barrel. Total black.

She said: they want to talk to you.

BLOW, GABRIEL

by ADAM WILSON

GABRIEL HAD ONE OF those old-fashioned landlines. He wound its cord around his finger while a voice on the other end relayed the instructions. The voice asked if he had questions. Gabriel did have questions—not about the instructions so much as the potential repercussions of carrying them out—but he sensed it would be impolitic to ask. Gabriel said he did not. He said he understood. Very well, said the voice.

Very well, said Gabriel.

When he hung up the phone, it gave a little ding. His mission was clear. He was to dust off his horn and usher back in the Lord.

* * *

Gabriel dragged himself up from the recliner where he'd spent the morning tuned to prayer. He had no way to answer—none of the angels could answer—but he still set his receiver to the symphony of suffering. He still considered it his duty. And perhaps he was naive or hopelessly old-fashioned, but Gabriel believed in some kind of osmosis through which he could absorb a certain portion of despair. He needed to believe, and so he carried that despair. It made him feel less lonely. He smoothed his slacks and stretched his atrophied wings. He put on a pot of coffee.

It was not a long drive to where he was going, a straight shot up the turnpike, five or six hours depending on traffic. The voice had stressed the situation's urgency, but Gabriel did not feel inclined to rush. Time moved differently here. Decades became centuries, which leaked into millennia. No one knew exactly when the Lord had left, but He'd been gone for long enough that few predicted his eventual return.

Gabriel sipped his coffee and drove at a leisurely pace. His cupholder was broken, so he balanced the thermos between his knees, careful not to let it tip when he leaned into the clutch. As he approached the city limits, he found himself passing the on-ramp for the turnpike. The byways offered a more scenic route to his destination. They would take him through sheep country, then shoot him out along the coast.

His hatchback struggled up the steeper hills, but Gabriel liked the mulchy scent of the air, and he was pleased to see some shepherds still roaming the pastures. And maybe it was the caffeine or the drop in elevation, but when the sea came into view on the final downhill straight, the magnitude of its beauty produced in him a sudden vertigo. His hands slipped from the wheel, and he flashed on an image of the hatchback gaining speed and spinning out into the surf. Gabriel managed to regain his composure. He downshifted into third and continued to drive.

It was coming on evening when Gabriel pulled over. He was only an hour from the base of the mountain, but he was tired. His task could wait until morning.

Earlier, the voice on the phone had assured Gabriel that when he stood atop the mountain and blew into his trumpet, the sound would reach the Lord in whatever alcove of the universe He currently occupied. The sound would signal the exigent necessity of His presence. He'd hear the clarion call and come Home.

Gabriel was less certain. In the past, his trumpet had been a conduit for the Lord's power. He himself had been a conduit. It stood to reason that, absent the Lord, they were artifacts, he and the horn.

And if, as Gabriel suspected, *nothing* happened when he put his lips to the mouthpiece? If the notes didn't soar? If their sound did *not* summon the missing Lord? Gabriel imagined himself on the mountain peak, solitary beneath the undiscriminating sun. The trumpet would slip from his sweating hands. The hope preserved in his innermost heart would be relinquished. Gone.

After securing a room at a roadside motel—a pink stucco relic called the Clamshell Motor Court—he went out in search of a drink. To meet the demands of a rapidly expanding population, developers had razed these little beach towns, replacing the old inns and taverns with corporate hotels. It was a miracle that a place like the Clamshell had survived the decimation, though the paucity of cars in its parking lot suggested that the motel's days were numbered.

On the upside, big hotels served liquor. Gabriel soon found himself at a patio table, a tumbler of whiskey in hand. At the beach bar behind him, a crowd had gathered to watch a basketball game. Gabriel could tell from the players' hairstyles and the lengths of their shorts that the game was an old one. There was no rhyme or reason to what came through the airwaves—programs from all eras and geographic locales. Some said it was the product of radio signals inadvertently traveling on the same band as prayer.

The specifics of the contest didn't matter; its viewers fell into a universal rhythm, silence punctuated by eruptions of cheer. There were no stars here, but the sky was silver-lit by a duo of moons who argued like siblings over the ebbs of the tide. Gabriel covered his drink with a coaster. Shoes in hand, he made his way to the shoreline. When the surf went out, his feet anchored themselves into the sand.

The Lord had been gone for so long that some wondered whether He'd been here at all. On certain days, even Gabriel doubted the veracity of his memories; those bygone years spent in His presence had taken on the hazy aura of a dream. But all of this—the sand, the sky, the ocean swell—who could deny that He'd built this place as surely as He'd built the earth below?

There was a third possibility, one that Gabriel didn't wish to entertain. He'd felt it there beneath the surface of this morning's phone call, the question he knew he couldn't ask. The possibility that he was not the only angel given this assignment. The possibility of six other angels. When Gabriel blew, they would hear it through the airwaves and follow suit. Seven blasts from seven horns. The destruction of all that He'd created would commence.

And who would be there to judge if this happened? Which souls, if any, would rise?

When Gabriel returned, there was a woman at his table. She asked if she could join him, despite already being seated. Gabriel said he didn't mind.

Bourbon? she said, indicating his drink.

What passes for it, said Gabriel.

I'm from bourbon country, said the woman. Then corrected herself: *Was* from bourbon country—I'm still getting used to being here.

The woman looked up at the moons: one waxing, one waning. Puzzle pieces that would never interlock. She lit a cigarette. Gabriel declined when she offered him one. To be honest, she said, I think I'm still in shock.

The woman was older than he first thought—perhaps nearing forty—but she showed none of the usual signs. She did not have the teeth of an addict or the sallow skin of the recently ill. And though she projected a melancholy air, he didn't take her for a suicide.

You're wondering how, she said.

I am, admitted Gabriel.

Giving life, the woman said.

It took him a moment to register her meaning. The hand holding her cigarette had started to tremble, and she used the other to steady it, guide it to her lips.

Gabriel said he was sorry. He had learned over time that this was all you could say. It did not suffice, but it was all. A silence followed. The woman smoked. Gabriel used a small straw to swirl the ice around his glass.

My baby, said the woman. I've been told he survived.

If he hadn't, said Gabriel. He'd be here with you now.

This did not appear to comfort the woman. She met Gabriel's eyes. You know things, she said. You must be a local.

Now he understood what she was doing at his table. The woman had clocked him. She thought he could help.

Some things, said Gabriel. As much as anyone does, I suppose.

I need to see my baby, said the woman. I need to see that he's all right.

Gabriel held out his palms. I'm sorry, he said again.

There must be some way of seeing, she said. The woman pointed at the game on TV. That's different, said Gabriel. No one understands how that works.

But this place, she said. The things we were told growing up.

The Lord—, he said.

I've heard, the woman said.

Gabriel considered telling her that those left behind would likely, one day, find themselves here. But he knew this was no consolation. She and her son would grieve this time apart. Each would be angry. The grief would come to define them. Even if they were to be reunited, an irrevocable sorrow would remain.

I'll take that cigarette now, Gabriel said.

Back in his room at the Clamshell, the woman asked to see his wings. Gabriel was self-conscious of his body, but he felt he owed her something. He unbuttoned his shirt and let it drop to the carpet. He'd long since shed his feathers, but the armature remained. He stretched his wings to the extent of their span.

The woman stared with neither revulsion nor awe. More bones, she said. More than I would have imagined. She asked if they hurt.

They get dry, said Gabriel.

There was lotion in the bathroom: white cream in a clam-shaped container. She rubbed it into his tertiary bones, which were thin and long like an umbrella's ribs. The lotion was cool. Gabriel could not remember the last time he'd been touched. He wondered, for a moment, if this was how it felt to receive human love.

Then he realized that the woman was crying. Her hands dropped from his body. A tear wet Gabriel's shoulder.

Am I being punished? the woman asked.

I don't believe that's possible, he said.

When he turned to console her, she covered her face with her hands. Over the airwaves, over the years, Gabriel had heard his share of weeping. But it was different in person. The woman brought her knees to her chest, and her body seemed to crumple. She made a bleating sound as she rapidly breathed.

Gabriel filled his rinse cup from the bathroom sink. Here, he said. Drink. It was warm in the room, so he turned on the fan. The gauze curtains lifted themselves from the window. The woman drank.

I'm being punished, she said.

Gabriel asked her: By whom?

He climbed the mountain in the midday sun. The incline was steep, and the path was overgrown with bunchgrass. Last night, he'd given the woman his bed, and now he felt the impact of sleeping on the carpet: a sore right hip and intermittent pain in his lower back. Gabriel's horn wasn't heavy, but its hard case was bulky and difficult to carry. He kept switching hands, and eventually settled on cradling the item to his chest with both arms as he shuffled along. Sweat dampened his shirt. He had to stop every few steps to catch his breath. He pushed on, fueled by his feeling of duty to the woman and by the anger he felt on her behalf.

At some point, more than halfway to the top, Gabriel rounded a thicket of shrubs to find a goat blocking his path. The goat was white, with large horns that looked crusted in dirt. At first it seemed to be staring at Gabriel, but when he inspected the animal's wide-set eyes, each appeared to point toward its periphery. His younger self might have read this as a sign, a message telling him to turn around and drive home. Maybe it was, but he would not be impeded. Gabriel grabbed a stick from the ground. He raised the stick to strike the goat, and the goat got up on its hind legs. Gabriel instinctively stepped backward, catching his shoe on a rock and turning his ankle. He cried out in pain and the goat ran off.

By the time he reached the apex, his ankle was swollen. He found a boulder to sit on and took off his shoes. He held his thermos to the swelling and looked out at the sea, the shore, the cars lined up on the turnpike. Souls arrived here by the second, he knew. Each day more than the last. They would continue to arrive.

Gabriel's eyes followed the path through the hills. Soon the pastures would be bulldozed just like the beach towns.

Condominiums would rise like mutant crops. Towering grids, all made of glass. Every window would be an eye, and behind every eye would sit a soul looking out.

Earlier, when Gabriel woke, he'd found the woman seated on the edge of the bed, holding his trumpet. The curtains were drawn, and the mountain could be seen in the distance, iridescent under the high morning sun. The woman looked focused, and Gabriel tried to remain silent and perfectly still. He watched her form a fist. The woman's hands were so small that her fist fit inside the trumpet's bell. She removed her hand. Holding the bell to her eye as if it were a telescope, she peered inside, into the dark.

Gabriel took the horn from its case. He raised himself atop the boulder to a standing position, putting most of his weight on the uninjured leg. In his mind, he heard the six other trumpets form a minor chord. He saw hail raining down upon cities, forests igniting in flame. Families fleeing to nowhere from lion-faced locusts as rivers ran bloody and darkness fell over the burning land. And when he pictured the souls floating up from the ashes, her infant son's was among them, a slow rising lace balloon. What would pass would pass. Gabriel inhaled through his nose and his body filled with breath. He put his lips to the mouthpiece and blew.

REDACTION

paintings by PERCIVAL EVERETT

Collage isn't new to me, but there is a different technique with these new paintings. The collage part is obscuring part of the picture you're seeing. It's present, but it's not available. That is what I mean by redaction. I am purposely making part of the image unavailable to the viewer in part because I'm interested in how we make stories. It's like in a novel: You don't know what happens to all the characters in the beginning of the novel. They exist someplace you can't see. You fill in those details as you read. As a writer, things don't exist unless I fill in the blanks on the page to tell that part of the story. That is what I mean when I talk about redaction and how that idea is related to these new paintings. For me to expect the viewer to see beyond what is present on a canvas, there must be something present that is not immediately visually available.

—*Percival Everett*

Redaction No. 1
2024
Oil on canvas
48 × 36 in.

Redaction No. 2
2024
Mixed media, collage on
archival paper
31.5 × 23.25 in.

Redaction No. 3
2024
Mixed media, collage on
archival paper
31.5 × 23 in.

Redaction No. 4
2024
Mixed media, collage on
archival paper
42.5 × 28.5 in.

Redaction No. 5
2024
Mixed media, collage on
archival paper
45 × 32.5 in.

Redaction No. 6
2024
Mixed media, collage on
archival paper
43 × 29 in.

Redaction No. 7
2024
Mixed media, collage on
archival paper
41.5 × 28.5 in.

Redaction No. 8
2024
Mixed media, collage on
archival paper
41.5 × 28.5 in.

Opposite:
Redaction No. 8 (detail)

Coracohyoid
Interhyoid
Hyoid Constr
Linea Alba
Flexor of Fi
SYSTEM

Redaction No. 9
2024
Oil on canvas
48 × 36 in.

Opposite:
Redaction No. 9 (detail)

Redaction No. 10
2024
Oil on canvas
36 × 29 in.

Redaction No. 11
2024
Oil on board
14 × 12 in.

Redaction No. 12
2024
Oil on board
14 × 12 in.

Redaction No. 13
2024
Oil on board
14 × 12 in.

Redaction No. 14
2024
Oil on board
14 × 12 in.

Redaction No. 15
2024
Oil on canvas
60 × 36 in.

Redaction No. 16
2024
Oil on canvas
60 × 36 in.

Redaction No. 17
2024
Mixed media, collage on archival paper
42.5 × 28.5 in.

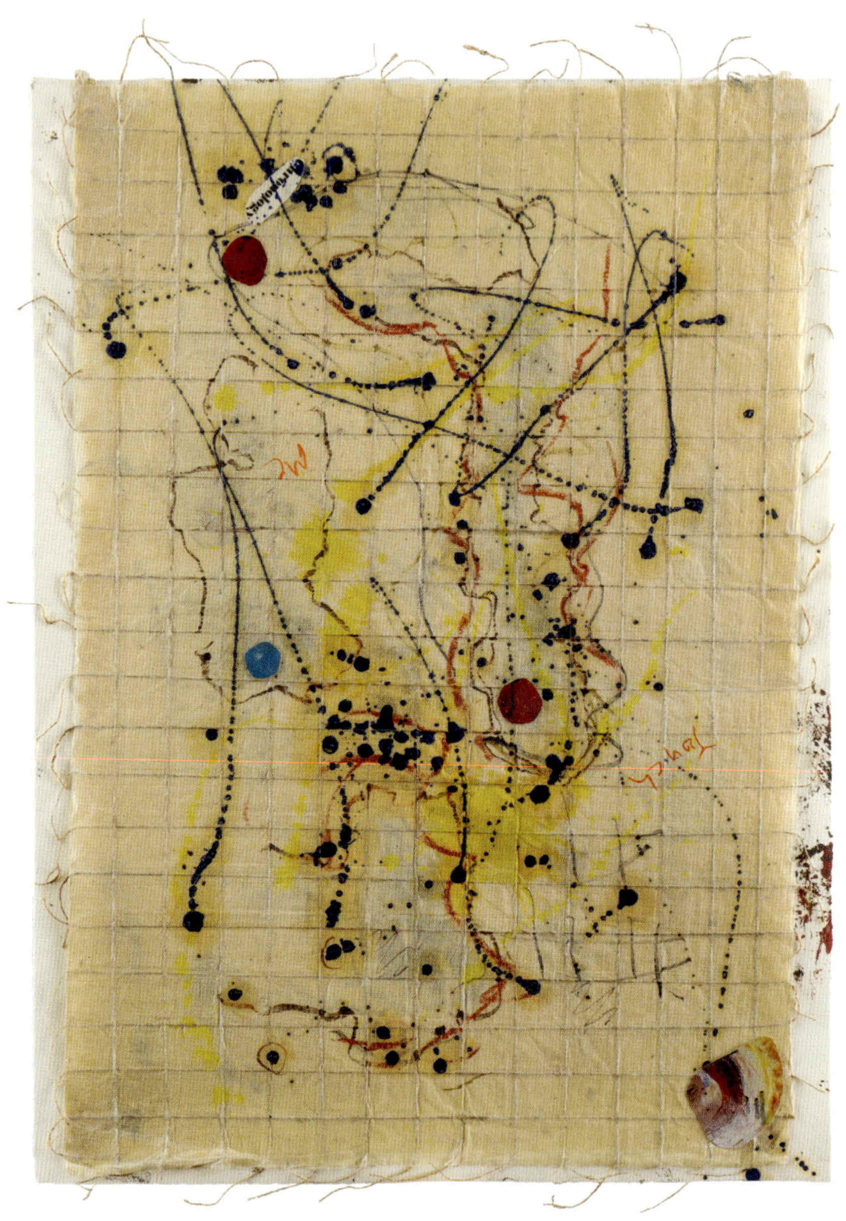

Redaction No. 18
2024
Mixed media, collage on
archival paper
45 × 32.5 in.

Redaction No. 19
2024
Mixed media, collage on
archival paper
42.5 × 28.5 in.

Redaction No. 20
2024
Oil on canvas
40 × 30 in.

HEART HOLE

by SOUVANKHAM THAMMAVONGSA

MY FRIEND TAUGHT AT the local college. I was his student. No one liked him very much. I think it was his jokes. He thought he was being funny, but to think him funny you would have to know him very well. The things he said made him come across as mean. I felt sorry for him, you could say. He just didn't know, and it didn't register.

After I graduated, I would drop by just to see how he was doing. He was old and alone. He reminded me of my dad. Tough and grumpy, but when you got to know him he wasn't that at all. We would go out to have lunch. Then dinners. We'd also go out to the movies sometimes. When I got married, I invited him to my wedding, and he baked a cake. His cakes were real special. He spent a lot of time on them. Never too sweet, and just soft enough.

Then, for my birthday one year, he came by with one of his cakes, and it just became a thing. I just expected it and didn't have to ask. He would just come over, like a parent, and then we'd put candles into the cake and light them up for me to blow out.

One evening, we had plans for dinner. At a Thai restaurant. They had this cheap buffet there. All you can eat for fifteen dollars a plate. This was before he met his husband and got married. He dressed in a suit like it was a date. I had just come from work and I was in a suit too.

We filled our plates with as much as we could. Pad thai, egg rolls, grilled chicken with lemongrass, stir-fry vegetables. When we sat down across from each other, we looked at each other's plates to see if the other got anything we missed.

We were having a great conversation, laughing loudly. I was just telling him about a new flower I got for my backyard. A bleeding heart. And that the petals. They really do look like a heart. There was a long pause after that, and for some reason, his eyes narrowed, and suddenly he raised his voice at me.

He said, "You fucking whore!"

He had never said anything like that to me before. Actually, no one had ever said that to me before. I was taken aback. I didn't know why he said that.

There was no reason to say that to me, at all, and even if there was, so what. Why should I be ashamed of that? The way he narrowed his eyes when he spoke made the space I took up shrink. He could have called me anything, really, and it would not have felt good said the way he said it. With such disgust.

The problem was it wasn't just him. It was that the people around us were looking. If you didn't know we were just friends, we could have looked like a couple on a date. An old man and a young woman. People assume things. Sexual things. I was the one with the ring and he wasn't. But why should I have to explain the situation to a room full of strangers, whom I probably would not ever see again?

I looked at my friend's face, looked for some relief to feel, but it never came. He remained serious, his face red, lips tight. Angry.

I thought he would add "Just kidding" loud enough so people in the room looking on at us would know it was a joke and that he wasn't serious. I started to chuckle. To show everyone in the room, it was a joke, nothing to look at over here. Get back to your dinners now. It was a good minute of laughing by myself, before his brows relaxed, his lips stretched across his face, and he joined me in laughing, too, to show that we were just kidding around.

Now, there are a lot of ways to tell jokes. You didn't have to involve the whole room, and it didn't have to be at my expense. We were not together, but the people at the restaurant didn't know that. Maybe I shouldn't have cared so much about what the people around us thought. They were strangers. Except I did care. It bothered me to be yelled at.

I don't know why he did that. And I never did ask him why. I didn't tell him it wasn't funny. He was my friend,

I thought. It was a joke. He hadn't meant to cause any harm by it.

After this, my friend soon met a man online. They moved in together and not long after got married. They bought a house together too. I couldn't come to the wedding, because I was out of town for work. That was okay, he said.

I met his husband, who was as tall as me, and we looked like we came from the same country, but we did not. Every time I saw his husband, his husband was always in the corner somewhere, smiling about something. So I assumed they were happy.

My friend was getting close to retiring. He was looking forward to it. He and his husband were fancy people. They liked skiing in France. I thought they would do that more now that he had the time. But he said his health wasn't so good.

He was exercising at home, pulling on an exercise band, when he passed out and fell face forward onto the floor and broke his nose. It was bruised up real bad. He had gone in to see a doctor about it, and they did tests, but nothing came up. They said he was healthy.

It wasn't until he had to get some routine dental surgery that they discovered something. An irregular heartbeat. Something about the way his heart was pumping. He had only one valve where there was normally two. His heart had to work overtime to pump it out of that one valve. There was a term for it, but I forget what he told me. I just remember thinking he was born that way. Missing a valve that was supposed to be there. And now there'd have to be a hole for that valve, where there was supposed to have been one already.

He had been in good health, good shape, so there was never any reason for him to look into his heart for anything unusual, he said.

Last week, he invited me over for dinner. He was on a wait list to get surgery. The doctors were going to put in a valve for him. Until he heard from the hospital, he had to take it easy. I didn't want to go visit him before his surgery, but he insisted. Besides, you know, in situations like this, you try to see a person any chance you get.

I didn't want him to go out of his way to make an elaborate meal like he usually does. He loved to cook. He liked to go all out to impress his guests. Shopping for ingredients all over the city, visiting specialty food stores just to get the things he needed. A jar of jam here. Roasted peanuts delivered only on Thursday afternoons. But that evening, he said he wasn't going to make anything that difficult.

"It's just pizza," he said.

The problem was it was not just pizza. He would culture his own yeast in his fridge for a few days. Spend hours beating the dough on his kitchen counter by hand. It would be physically demanding. I told him to get premade dough, but he wouldn't hear of that.

When I got to their place, he was in the kitchen, putting on the toppings. I breathed a sigh of relief. That his heart hadn't given out while trying to make dinner. Mushrooms, arugula, and some cured meat he smuggled back on a trip from Italy.

We greeted each other and when the conversation turned to him, he said, "Last week, I passed out on the kitchen floor. And *this guy*," pointing accusingly at his husband, "didn't even bother to call me an ambulance!"

I didn't know if it was true. It would be just the kind of joke he would tell. I was waiting for it. For him to tell me it was a joke. And to be sorry.

His husband stood there in the kitchen grinning. He had big white teeth. He has the same grin no matter what is happening to him—his birthday or his favorite song on the radio came on or he saw a rainbow—so I didn't know what this grin meant.

I said, "You came out all right though? You seem fine to me, standing here."

"Well, when I came to, I called my doctor and he told me to go to the emergency room to get it checked out, and to get myself a defibrillator in case it happens again." He pointed to the defibrillator, and I looked over there at the wall. I wondered how much it cost to have one.

When the pizza was cooked, we went into the dining room and ate it. We were sitting there, each quietly taking bites. I asked him to pass the salt and he did. I watched the salt fall onto my pizza slice like snow. It was so white and sparkly. And then it disappeared into the warmth of the cheese.

My friend said, suddenly, to his husband, "*Why* didn't you call an ambulance?" bringing up what happened when he passed out. It seemed like a private conversation he and his husband should have, and I didn't know the point of bringing it up now, while I was there.

His husband grinned, and said, "Because I was giving you CPR!"

"Ah, you just want nothing but my money," he said bitterly. His head sank between his shoulders. "You stand to inherit so much! You just want it all and to start yourself a new life. That's what you want isn't it!"

It reminded me of the time we were at the restaurant years ago. I recognized that look. The way his husband was looking at me, like he wanted to explain himself, but didn't know if I really needed to know all that.

I thought, "So what! He's your husband. He should inherit all that you have." There shouldn't be any shame in taking everything someone left you when they're gone. When you are gone, that's it! You are gone. You don't get a say in what happens after. You don't get to take it all with you.

But I didn't say that.

"Just joking," my friend said.

Except that I didn't think it was a joke. He was angry, probably, that he wasn't as healthy as he wanted to be. That he waited so long, saving up his money all these years, waiting for retirement, and he couldn't go skiing like he had planned for, because it was too much for his heart.

I decided then that I didn't want to be friends with him anymore. I didn't like his jokes. I tolerated them before because I thought he was lonely and sad, and maybe not being with someone for a while, he forgot what was funny to him might not be funny to someone outside of him. I could see now what it was. He was just plain mean.

Over the years, he hadn't been much of a friend either. When I got divorced, he said, "What are you thinking? I hope you know what you are doing." And when I told him why, he said, "That's fairy-tale thinking. All relationships end up that way."

A few days ago, he texted me to say the hospital scheduled his surgery. I never answered. I wanted to text him back and tell a joke the way he would tell one, but it wasn't funny, and I couldn't go near the kind of mean he could make.

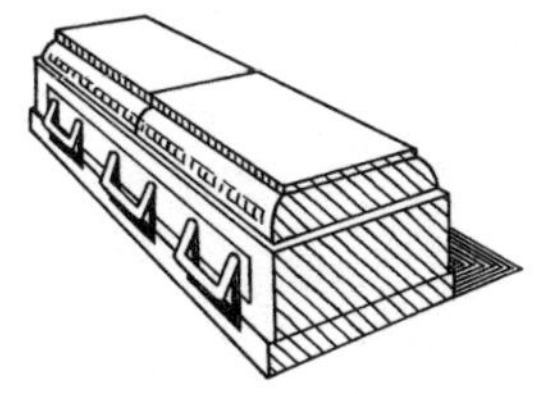

A CONVERSATION WITH MY UNCLE

(IN WHAT MIGHT BE PURGATORY)

by KEVIN JOHNSTON

Me: What happens now?

Now? Or *now*?

Both?

The *now* is probably a bit too much for you to handle.

Okay.

But *now*? Lowercase? It's just us talking.

Okay.

You'll have to do this with everyone.

Everyone?

Everyone here.

What will we talk about?

We're going to talk about how you've used me as a party trick.

What?

When you talk about my death.

I was only a kid when you died.

I was murdered.

I know.

You do. It's what you tell everyone when you run out of things to say.

That's not—

It's your big reveal.

I'm sorry.

I'm not angry.

Good.

But we have to talk about it.

Okay.

Why do you think I was murdered?

I don't know.

But you have an idea.

I think you were murdered because you got involved with the wrong people.

And?

And they killed you.

Maybe.

Maybe.

Yet you tell everyone what you think happened as if it's fact.

I'm sorry.

You already said that.

Are you sure you're not mad?

I am.

Sure or mad?

I'm not mad. I just want to know why.

Why I tell the story of your murder?

What compels you to.

I don't know.

It's not sadness. When your dog died, that was sad. You tell that story when you want to show your compassion, that you can feel.

It was sad when Bentley died.

And my death? What are you saying with that story? That you're dangerous?

What?

That you have an edge or something?

I… I have to do this with everyone?

Everyone here.

You know I go past the old house sometimes.

It's still there?

You didn't know that?

It's complicated. It's not like the movies.

Tony bought it.

He did?

He's doing okay. Great, actually.

Really?

I'm confused.

It's hard to explain.

Can you try?

We don't have time.

I didn't expect to be a pallbearer at your funeral.

I didn't expect to die.

We were all surprised.

Except for your mother.

She didn't think you would get murdered.

But she always knew something would happen.

She didn't think you were like the rest of them.

You say "them" as if we all aren't the same family. As if my parents aren't your grandparents.

That's always the way it felt. Do you know when she'll die?

Your mother?

Yes.

I only live here. I don't run the place.

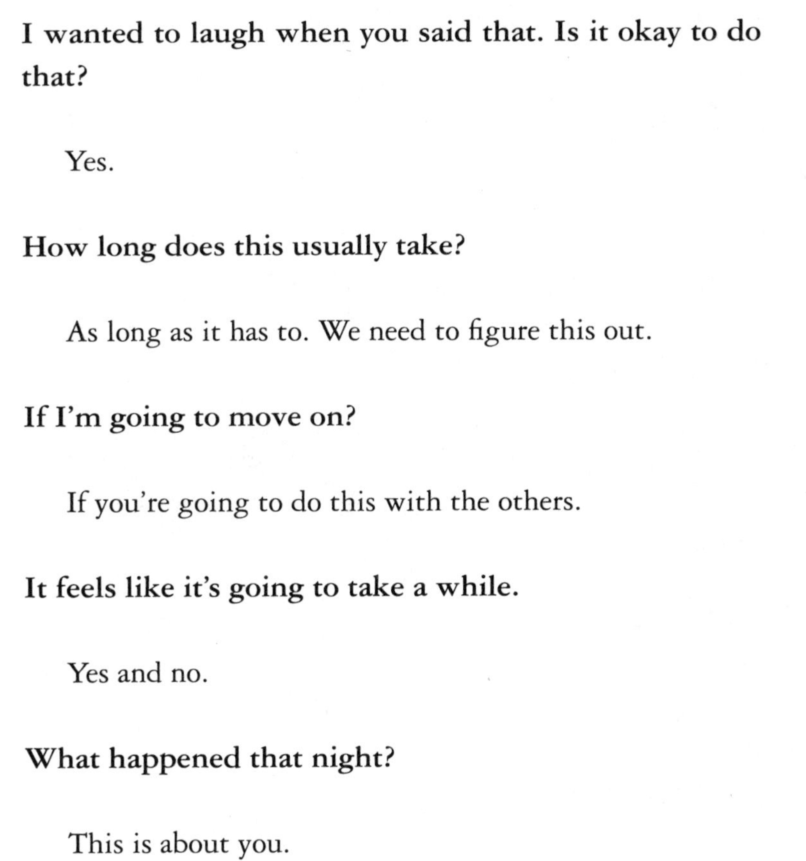

I wanted to laugh when you said that. Is it okay to do that?

Yes.

How long does this usually take?

As long as it has to. We need to figure this out.

If I'm going to move on?

If you're going to do this with the others.

It feels like it's going to take a while.

Yes and no.

What happened that night?

This is about you.

Did you know the people who did it?

We're here for you, not me.

Did it hurt?

Yes.

I'm sorry.

[*Protracted silence*]

Why did it happen?

Why don't you tell me?

I wasn't there.

Yet when you tell the story, you make it very clear that someone held me down and put a gun to my head. That I was killed for not paying my debts.

Aren't we all?

You're being glib? About my murder? Here?

I'm sorry.

There's too much work to do.

Okay.

Okay.

But I don't know what to do.

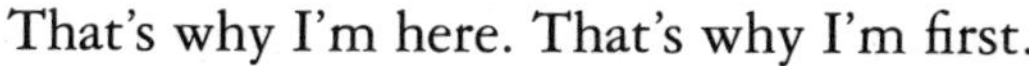

That's why I'm here. That's why I'm first.

First?

I told you. You have to see everyone.

Right.

But first, it's me.

So, what's next?

We need to get to the bottom of this.

Of what?

Of why you've made my story your own. What do you think happened that night? Why do you think I was killed?

I don't know.

I asked what you think.

I think you owed people money.

And?

You took too long to pay. Maybe you weren't going to pay, and they knew it.

Why do you think that?

Because you gambled. A lot.

And?

I saw the people you hung around with.

You were just a kid.

Kids know a lot more than adults think they do.

Fair enough.

And I heard my mom on the phone talking to the police the night you died.

You believe what you heard?

I did.

Do you believe it now?

I don't know.

Did you believe it yesterday?

Yes.

But now you don't know?

You broke her heart, you know.

Who?

My mother.

My sister.

Yes.

But she saw it coming.

She did.

She did.

But she won't talk about it. Not anymore. Not that it happened. Not that she saw it coming.

No?

Can we keep going?

You can't rush this.

Okay.

Why tell this story to people you barely know?

We did this part.

I'm not satisfied with your answer.

I don't know the real answer.

That's a start.

But what's the finish?

Don't worry about that.

Should I be scared?

Maybe.

That's not comforting.

We're not here for comfort.

What are we here for?

Answers.

About your death?

Murder.

About your murder?

No.

About why I talk about it?

About why you use it.

What do I use it for?

That's what we're here to figure out.

What if there's no reason?

There's always a reason.

You seem certain.

This isn't my first rodeo.

Since when do you say things like that?

"First rodeo"?

Yes. Like *rodeo*. We're from Queens.

It's different here. That stuff doesn't matter.

Does it feel strange to say "This isn't my first rodeo"?

Why?

It isn't you.

You know who I am?

I know who you're not.

Tell me.

You're not a guy who should have been murdered.

Okay.

You're not a guy who should have fallen into all that.

Why?

Because you are smart.

Smart people get murdered too.

True. Do you blame yourself?

It's complicated.

Do you feel guilty?

Unequivocally.

I'm not sure you're a guy who says "unequivocally" either.

I do now.

Fair enough.

So, that's who I'm not. Who do you think I am?

A Son. A Father. An Uncle. A Brother.

But that's all default. I didn't have a choice.

Okay.

So, what do you think I am?

A bit broken? Maybe?

Good. A beginning.

I don't think it was your fault.

Doesn't matter.

It does.

Why?

Because I don't think you had a choice.

About what happened?

About what the world did to you. Before that night.

Others went through worse.

Maybe they were better equipped.

Maybe. I didn't have to do the things I did.

That applies to everyone.

Some of the things I did were really bad.

And others did worse.

That can't be the measure.

But maybe it is.

It isn't.

So, what is it?

We're here for you, not me.

It feels like a lot of this is about you.

It's not.

Yet it is.

I don't want to argue with you.

I'm happy to see you.

I'm happy to see you too.

I miss your laugh.

I miss laughing.

I can't tell if this is even real.

It is.

I believe you.

But we have to finish.

I know.

What else?

That's an unfair question.

I know, but try.

I never thought it would be you.

Why?

You were the good one.

My brothers are good people too.

Not like you. And I'm not sure that's true.

I'm not the good one.

Maybe just better?

But still not good.

It just never felt like you. It felt like maybe all the stuff you saw happened so often that it just became normal, even though it was anything but.

It feels like cheating to say that might be true.

Why?

You're supposed to be the one answering the questions.

Okay.

So, let's try again.

Okay.

Why do you think you use my story the way you do?

You never said "use" before.

Yes, I did.

I must have forgotten.

You have.

Do you think I'm using you?

The story, not me.

I see.

I'm sorry if that hurts to hear.

I know you don't mean to hurt me.

Yes, that's true.

I think it's because I miss you.

But that's not what you say when you tell the story. That's not what it feels like.

How do you know how I feel?

Don't be defensive.

I feel put on the spot.

You are. It's time for answers.

Well, can't you at least help me?

I'm helping you by asking questions.

Ask me again.

Why do you think you tell my story?

Maybe I'm afraid I'm not interesting.

But my death is?

You were murdered.

And?

Did you know them?

They were familiar faces.

That sounds like something out of a movie.

Is that why you tell the story?

Did you ask them not to do it?

Not to kill me?

Yes.

Not at first.

Why?

Because I didn't think they actually would.

Really?

I thought I could talk my way out of it.

What happened when you realized you couldn't?

I begged them not to kill me.

What did you say?

I told them about your aunt and your cousins. How they would be alone.

What did they say?

They said it was too late for that.

Were you scared?

I don't remember.

Are you lying to me?

To both of us.

I'm sorry.

The waiting was the worst. Once I knew it was going to happen.

I can't even imagine.

When you know it's going to happen, you shrink into something you don't recognize.

Did you have a moment of acceptance?

I'm not a monk.

I know.

If you make it back, tell them I'm sorry?

I can go back?

Maybe.

I thought it was all over.

Did *you* have a moment of acceptance?

No.

See? We all fight until the end.

This feels more like a beginning.

For you or me?

Both, in different ways.

Fair enough.

I guess.

But we need an answer. They're going to want that.

Who?

Focus.

I tell your story because it's the most interesting thing about me.

The most interesting thing about you is that I was murdered?

It was like after 9/11.

What's that got to do with it?

Everyone wanted to say they lost someone so they could feel closer to the tragedy.

Everyone except someone who actually lost someone.

Exactly.

We all lost something that day.

True.

This is different.

And the same.

But why tell people you barely know?

It's the look on their face.

Like a card trick.

You're making me feel bad.

That's not the goal.

But it's still happening.

Well, why do you think you feel bad?

Maybe I shouldn't be telling your story.

Now we're getting somewhere.

Maybe only you know the real truth.

The real truth?

You know what I mean.

I don't.

Your version of it.

There's only one version.

Of the truth?

Yes.

So maybe it's the only way I can tell it.

Maybe.

Maybe I don't actually know what happened that night.

Okay.

And maybe I shouldn't pretend like I do.

Okay.

That felt like something.

Like what?

Like a confession?

Now we're getting somewhere.

Maybe.

You're getting there.

But I'm still not sure why.

I know.

Are we closer?

That's up to you.

I want people to know I'm not like you.

Most of them wouldn't even know I existed unless you told them.

True.

Then why tell them?

To show them what I could be. What I came from.

What do you come from?

A mess.

That's a bit harsh, no?

I mean, my mother ran as far away from all of you as she could.

She did. We all saw it.

But I get it.

I worried she hated us.

She always had a soft spot for you.

I'm glad.

But she had to get away.

Do you think that's why you feel the way you feel?

She helped shape the way I see you and your brothers, but I made up my own mind.

They're not just my brothers, they're your uncles. Was she ashamed?

I think for a long time she was, but eventually, she let it go.

Are you ashamed of me?

No.

But you're driven to talk about me.

I just want to finish this. Whatever it is.

It's not a linear conversation.

I don't know how to finish the story.

Do you think this is a story?

Maybe.

That it's not real?

Maybe.

I assure you it's real.

That sounds menacing.

It's not intended to be.

Then what's the point of saying it?

To make you understand that this is serious.

I know this is serious.

They're going to need an answer.

Who are they?

Focus. Please.

I've given you an answer.

But you haven't.

We're spinning in circles.

And eventually we'll stop.

When?

When you—

Give you an answer?

Yes.

What do you want me to say?

That's not how it works.

Then how does it work?

You're thinking about more than you have to right now.

I want to know what's at stake.

Everything.

You're being dramatic.

I'm not.

I want to leave.

I'm afraid that isn't possible.

Ever?

Right now.

Even if I answer the question?

I don't know.

So, what's the point of answering the question?

There are others to speak with.

What if I just refuse?

Then we'll sit here forever.

Forever?

Yes.

Am I dead?

Not exactly.

What does that mean?

You just need to give me your answer.

You're getting impatient.

I have a job to do.

What's the rush?

There is no rush.

Then why the pressure?

I want you to see.

But then what happens?

You're too focused on what happens next.

Can't you tell me? I don't like this.

You don't have to like it. You just have to answer the question.

What's wrong with the answers I've given you?

Only you know the answer to that.

But I don't.

You do. You have to dig.

What?

Ask yourself. Not for me. For yourself.

Can it be two things?

Sure.

Well, let's talk about the first.

Okay.

It's exciting.

My death?

Your murder.

Yes.

It's a shocking story. Especially in the world I live in now.

How so?

This kind of thing doesn't happen to the people I know.

What kind of thing?

People getting killed for not paying their debts.

You don't know that's the case.

Just tell me the truth. It'll make it easier for me to answer.

What do you want to hear?

The truth.

What if it's at odds with what you've been saying?

I'll deal with it.

Okay.

Okay what?

You were right. You are right.

About what?

About why I was killed.

Murdered.

Yes.

You owed money.

Because I owed money too often.

And couldn't pay?

That was a big part of the problem.

Why didn't you come to us?

You were just a kid.

The family.

You can only ask so many times.

But what if you told them they were going to kill you?

I told them that before.

And you were still around.

And I never really believed it.

You thought you could talk your way out of it.

I did.

And you couldn't.

I couldn't.

Thank you for telling me the truth.

Thank you for listening.

It sounds like I was right.

Somewhat, but we're here to find out why you're telling the story.

This again.

Was it to shock people?

Maybe I was just trying to play to the room. Be the center of attention.

I don't think so.

Like I said, I guess I just wanted to prove I'm not like you.

And more like your mother.

Maybe.

She was always trying to get away.

It's why we kept moving.

She made it literal.

She wasn't actually ashamed of you, you know.

A bit embarrassed?

Something like that. But it wasn't about you.

It wasn't?

It was about her.

How so?

About creating her own life.

Away from us.

Away from all that came with you.

What came with us?

Come on.

I'm not saying it was great.

Okay.

But I need you to say what it was.

The yelling. The theatrics. The secrets.

It was tough.

She never blamed you.

Who did she blame?

No one, not really. She just wished it could have been better.

Me too.

She liked you best.

That's nice to hear.

It hurt her when you died. Worse than the others' deaths.

I was the first.

That's not why.

I know.

Good.

Who do you blame?

Me?

There's no one else here.

Except everyone.

That comes later.

I don't blame anyone.

Really?

Maybe I blame the world.

Why?

Because things are the way they are. Maybe it isn't anyone's fault.

You don't wish things were different?

That's another question altogether.

How so?

A wish isn't blame. I wish it was different, but I don't know that it's anyone's fault.

There's always someone to blame.

I don't think that's true.

At all?

Maybe it's the world. Maybe it's the way we were all built inside of it.

That's a lot of maybes.

I'm new here.

This is true. And we should stay on track.

Okay.

What's the second reason?

I think—

No more thinking.

I guess—

Nope.

I'm trying to prove I'm not like you.

Why?

Why am I not like you?

No. Why are you trying to prove it?

Because I'm not so sure it's true.

That sounds like a second thing.

It might be.

Maybe the story isn't for them. It's for you.

I think they should put us all in a lineup.

I don't like lineups.

In a row.

Why?

You might not even know we were from the same family.

How so?

We look different. We speak differently. We do different things.

But everyone is different.

That's true. But we don't feel the same.

Yet?

What is that a result of?

You tell me.

The distance we purposely put between us.

And?

The way my mom used you, all of you, as examples of what not to do.

She was ashamed.

No.

Really?

Maybe embarrassed.

Okay.

But that was then. Now, I'm here. Having this conversation with you.

And?

I'm scared.

This can be overwhelming.

It's not this I'm scared of.

Then what?

That I'll turn out to be like the rest of you.

Why?

I don't want to blame my mom.

Then don't.

She was more like you than she thought. More than she wanted to be.

I agree.

Maybe the way she distanced herself was more window dressing than anything else.

I don't understand.

The things she did were to telegraph who she was and wasn't to the world.

And you?

I think I'm more detached from you than my mother is, but I am also just like her, so I don't know.

You are one of us. Part of this family.

I am. But I worked so hard to lose the accent.

What accent?

Come on. What accent?

I mean it.

When I was a kid, my mom told me that if I grew up and sounded like the rest of the family, everyone would think I was dumb.

I don't sound dumb.

I didn't say you did.

Are you sure she didn't hate us?

I don't know what to say except that she didn't. I know that.

I'm not so sure.

It's complicated.

Hate?

No. Deciding how you feel about where you came from.

Is there a choice?

For some of us.

So, what's your choice? How do you feel about where you came from?

It's complicated.

How so?

It's changed over the years.

How?

It was different when I was younger. I was trying to prove something.

What?

That I wasn't like you.

I—

Not just you. The whole family.

You don't have to spare my feelings.

It's the truth.

Okay.

I was afraid people would think I was like the rest of the family.

Is it that bad?

In some ways.

So, what is this really about then?

It's about how I wanted to be different.

You are.

But when I was younger, I wasn't so sure.

You did have something to prove.

To myself.

And now?

I learned more than I thought I did from you.

Yet you're different.

Yes, but that doesn't mean I'm anti—

Or pro.

It's not about the family.

Nothing exists in a vacuum.

I guess it's just different.

Why?

Because I think it shaped who I am.

It did.

I feel lucky to have grown up with a foot in two worlds. To understand them.

You talk about us like a scientist. Like you're doing research.

I don't mean to.

She pulled you away too early.

And she also othered you.

More lab talk.

I never felt connected to any of you. You all felt like someone else's family.

Something to endure.

Oof.

We are here to find the truth.

I still loved all of you.

Past tense?

I don't know what tense to use. I don't even know where we are.

We're on the precipice of the truth.

Who's the philosopher now?

Don't deflect.

Fair.

Keep going.

The truth is it wasn't about you.

Okay.

The truth is I used your story to be whatever I needed it to be.

Which was?

To get attention. To show I was different. A story to show where I came from. A story to show I was adjacent to something dangerous. A story to show that I had endured a tragedy.

It seems so malleable.

It was a malleable story.

But it wasn't. It was a murder. They came to my house with a gun, and it wasn't for show. I didn't have the money I owed the guy they worked for, and it wasn't the first time. They told me that there wouldn't be a next time. I begged them not to kill me. Then one of them put the gun to my head, and I wept like a child. The last thing I remember was the loudest noise I'd ever heard. It felt like it was inside my head. Maybe I flinched or maybe I just died.

I—

Don't cry.

I can't help it.

That's what actually happened. Whether it's mine or yours or anyone else's.

Thank you for telling me the details.

Stop crying.

I'm sorry.

I forgive you.

Why?

Because I can.

What happens next?

That's not up to me.

Am I dead?

Something like that.

I don't remember dying.

I'm sure you don't.

But you told me about everything when you died.

I didn't remember everything at first. And I still only

remember everything up to that moment. I think they want it like that.

Who is "they"?

I don't actually know.

But like they with a capital *T*?

Very much so.

What do they look like?

I've never seen them.

Then how do you know they exist?

I don't.

Then what are we doing?

What we're told.

This is crazy.

Maybe. But it's all we can do.

Okay. Then what's left?

Everyone else.

Everyone? I don't think I can do this.

You can.

Why?

Because you have to.

THE RIFF

by ASHLEY NELSON LEVY

DEB'S HUSBAND CALLED ME at work, and seeing his name on the screen, I knew: Deb's dead. I'm not sure at what age surprises become proof of inevitable disaster, and disasters proof of your foresight. But as it turned out, Deb wasn't dead, and her husband hadn't meant to call me. One of the kids had been playing with the phone again. I listened to Deb's husband take the phone back into his possession, worried about who had been conjured. "Oh, just you," he said. This also came as a surprise since, in the fifteen years they'd been married, Deb's husband and I had never had that level of intimacy, or any. When I tried to be honest with myself about why I'd never liked him, I could come up with only two things: He wasn't a serious person, and he had taken Deb away from me. He thought I was an elitist, though that wouldn't have been the word he'd used. He said Deb wasn't home just then, but if I wanted, he could have her call me later. The generous gatekeeper. I hadn't talked to Deb, the person I called my best friend, in over six months. I said sure and wondered if he would relay the message. More than that, I wondered if Deb would call if she received it.

Sometimes life bundles these odd, unrelated surprises together to try to make a miracle happen. This sounds like it should be embroidered somewhere, but it's true. The same day of the phone call, my job asked me to travel to Rome. Later I went home and pulled a book from the shelf and noticed the framed photo that sat next to it. Deb and I are twenty-something in the photo, biking around a piazza with dresses and skirts hiked over our thighs. I don't remember who took the picture. I don't remember most people outside the frame from that year. Only Deb and I are in focus.

So I texted her about the upcoming trip, and then, holding my breath a little, I wrote: *Come with me and we'll go to Florence.* Even though Deb and I were far from each other—psychically far, that is, geographically we lived only ninety suburban minutes apart—I couldn't imagine returning without her after all this time; the memory of the city was bound in the memory of her. Deb wrote back right away, and after a few nostalgic exchanges, she told me that, if she could afford to, she would be there in a heartbeat. Then I offered to pay in full for the trip, and after a dramatic, twenty-four-hour pause, she responded that, while grateful, she could not accept. I wondered if the offer to pay was some sort of irreparable mistake. I tried to keep the thread going to gauge whether this was so. But then the micro demands of our lives abruptly ended the conversation, and after I relayed all of this to my husband, he asked if he could take the trip with me instead.

So I left the kids with my parents and finally saw Florence again, this time with John. It felt crazy not to stop in Florence if I was already going all the way to Italy, but without Deb, it also felt like a transgression. There was so much to revisit—the churches with the Giottos and Masaccios, that restaurant with the pear-stuffed ravioli—but I also didn't want to leave the kids for too long. As a concession to the children and somehow also to Deb, I only allowed myself two days, mostly to see the building where she and I had lived, inseparably, just a block from the Bargello. I booked a guided museum tour at the Uffizi, which embarrassed me more than I was willing to admit. Why? I felt above it, was why, having lived there, wanting more authentic access to the city, to feel again the lightness or perhaps even the weightiness of life at twenty years old. I wanted this while knowing that cities change and belonged to no one, especially those who leave them.

I was twenty the year we lived in Florence, she was twenty-three. It was a time in our lives when two and a half years made a difference. She had slept with more people, she had traveled alone, she kept an Oyster card in her wallet from her one trip to London. I thought this was the classiest thing in the world, that she had a card ready for the Tube in her pocket. There was a soft trail of freckles across her nose and cheeks, the kind that I see girls at my daughters' school paint on their faces these days, as if freckles were the thing all girls wished to have. But her hair was her thing. It was voluminously black with riotous curls and what I looked for in a crowded room if I lost her. Years later, when we lived together in San Francisco, she came home from a haircut with it styled straight and flat, and I cried at the sight of it. She'd rolled her eyes, annoyed, as if I were holding her back from transformation, but there was a part of her that loved it too. That loved feeling known any which way. I retreated to my room. Later she followed me there with her hair dripping all over my sheets to show me she'd washed out the imposter.

On the train from Rome to Florence, I listened to a language app while John, my husband, slept across from me. The app was called Ciao, Baby! and I realized as I watched my partner's mouth go slack that I should have opted for the paid version. This free Ciao, Baby! was a loop of fractured vocabulary that would leave me helpless in the face of conversation, though it did provide an accurate account of a tourist's passage through Italy: *How much?, I need the bathroom, delicious!, goodbye.* As we pulled into Santa Maria Novella station, I saw that if I had scrolled further in the app store, I would have found Ciao, Baby!'s legitimate sibling, Buongiorno, Italia, which had 150K more reviews and two additional stars. I began to feel depressed about my lost relationship to the language, one I'd worked so hard at so many years ago. But Deb, had she been there, would have reminded me that the Italians we'd spent our nights with wanted to practice their English to better woo gals like us, and that we never worked as hard at cultural integration as I'd told myself. That year, we'd worked hard on other things, like shaking our ass at the club and roaming the worn cobblestones as if our feet were the first to ever tread them.

John and I checked into a hotel called Brunelleschi's Palace, where the staff apologized profusely when I opened the lobby door myself. The ceilings were painted with dead noblemen, and a woman sat on a Savonarola chair with a morning glass of white wine near the elevators, girdled by designer shopping bags. For a brief moment the woman looked like Deb, and I had the insane fantasy that she had hopped on a flight at the last minute to surprise me. But of course it was not Deb. Deb would not stay at a place like this, now or ever. Staying at a place like this with Deb would have embarrassed me. And it occurred to me as I approached the desk that I might have taken the excess too far to numb the botched expectations for this trip. *You know what might make you feel better about missing your girlfriend?* I imagined my subconscious saying. *A palace.*

"Buongiorno," I said, a little too grandly. I parroted verse from the accommodations chapter of Ciao, Baby!, hopefully describing our reservation and how long we planned to stay. The man at the desk wore a captain's hat. "Wonderful, signora," he said in English. "Here is your touristic map."

We lunched at a place recommended by the map, where the food was good but overpriced. The restaurant with the pear-stuffed ravioli, as it turned out, no longer existed, and the windows were dark in another trattoria I'd wanted to try. John overordered. Instead of telling him to order less I insisted he get what he liked while mentally tallying the bill.

"You're barely touching your food," I said.

"I think I picked up a little something in Rome," he said, daintily clearing his throat.

I sipped my wine. While I'd spent four days in a hotel conference room in Rome, John had frequented every Roman museum and café, no doubt picking up something while he enjoyed himself. It was the same deal I'd offered Deb—company in exchange for money—and I wasn't sure why it bothered me when John had swapped himself in. It was unfair to transfer my disappointment over Deb to John, but it really should have been her on this trip. Our chance to reconnect. John honked his nose into the cloth napkin and asked where I wanted to go next.

"My old apartment," I said, checking my email.

"Get off that thing."

"In a minute."

"You only make things worse for yourself," John said, as I pecked a response. "You set the expectation that you never really take a vacation."

He had, of course, no idea about my world, the expectation. It was impossible not to wonder how the younger me might also judge the woman sitting here now: a female executive who, as of late, seemed to identify only with the villains in the movies she watched from business class, women accompanied by dark, menopausal theme music when encountering the young heroines in heat.

My husband was in the same line of utilitarian work, but our careers did not run in parallel. I held the more senior position, making double his salary, which often seesawed the feeling of advantage between us—power on my side, freedom on his.

"You're right," I said, putting the phone down.

"I haven't looked at my work email since we left."

"Hm."

All my female colleagues were in the same position, earning more than their male counterparts. But none of us ever talked about this. Was this progress? I wanted to know what Deb would say. I couldn't remember what exactly her husband did, only that she was often lamenting the state of their finances; her office job did not produce the salary mine did. These days it could take her weeks to return a phone call, reminding me where I fell in the pecking order. But Deb had always been like that. Hot and cold—not with people, necessarily, but with life. When she was hot, she would burn like the brightest star in the sky and there was no end to the evening and everyone would bask in that brilliance. We would feel more brilliant, more awake ourselves. She had that way with people. But when she was cold the world went gray with her, food tasted drier, the jokes useless. When we lived together, I maintained a rare access to her regardless of how the thermometer ran, which made me feel more important than any other achievement in my life. But now that we lived in separate houses, separate cities, with separate families and separate lives, I had just as hard a time getting to her as anyone else, and, for years, this had made me mercurial too. As soon as I would make peace with my love for her and the limitations of what she could give in return, she would no-show to my kid's birthday, she would forget to call me on mine. And then my love would feel like a cloud, a poison, and it would take everything in me not to scream into her voicemail that people couldn't live on history alone.

Only once in the last few years had I felt close to her in the way we once were. Deb had lost a pregnancy in her second trimester and asked me to come stay, and I took a previously unthinkable week off. It felt strange, the first few nights, to send her off to bed with someone else, her husband, while I retreated to the twin in the spare room down the hall. On the second-to-last night of my visit, Deb appeared in my room at some dark hour, sliding tightly next to me under the sheets, saying nothing, in the way we once slept, deeply and peacefully. When I woke in the morning, she was gone. Sitting with her now, I would have wanted to tell her over a bottle of wine that John and I had been going through a riff, that "the riff" was the private name I'd given it, taken from an acronym at work: RIF, a reduction in force. *We lost her in the RIF*, people would say ominously, as if the word were a war that the company could not help or prevent. The longer I'd worked in corporate, the more I'd realized how incapable people were of saying what they meant, unable to speak aloud the full names of bad things for fear it would find them. The parallel between the work RIF and the riff in my marriage was that the split seemed unrelated to performance. No one had cheated, no one had been cruel. We had merely become redundant to each other.

Bullshit, Deb would have said. *People don't split the sheets over nothing.*

I couldn't remember the exact number of our old building, but I knew our street. I insisted on finding it without using my phone. I was slightly self-conscious of the way I narrated for John as we walked: This was the old women's prison; this was the best local bar; this was Santa Margherita de' Cerchi, where it was said Dante first met Beatrice; this was a place where I'd liked to dance. I did not say: Deb and I slept with the brothers that bartended there; Deb carried me home from that place one night, my face buried in the scent of her hair; we snuck in the coatroom of that club once and put our hands in every pocket. I couldn't tell if that version of me felt like the ghost or if the current version of me did, dead and performing a life review. I was also aware as we walked that longing for a younger, more vibrant version of yourself was the easiest cliché one could stumble upon in midlife. But how not to want to taste the sweetness of youth every now and again? So what if memory has extracted the bitterness?

We wandered along the narrow streets until we came to the front of a large wooden door crowned by an iron fleur-de-lis. "This is it," I said to John, slightly breathless, and as I approached he snapped my picture. It was eighty-eight steps to our floor, Deb and I had counted. I was about to text her a picture when something occurred to me. I walked another twenty feet down the street. Was this the one? Now I couldn't tell. I was certain there had been one neighbor separating our building from the side street that cut perpendicular.

I looked at the top floor, scanning the windows, one of which we'd always had open just to hear the sounds from the street. A dizziness came over me, maybe from the wine at lunch. My body felt light, then suddenly leaden. I caught John staring at me with concern.

"Well, it was one of these," I said.

We walked along the river as John went through a pack of tissues. I'd wanted to head to Piazzale Michelangelo for views of the city, but it was clear my traveling companion really wasn't well. We could go tomorrow, he suggested, we still had a full morning before the Uffizi tour. So we looped back over to the other side of the water, through Piazza della Repubblica, stopping briefly at the San Lorenzo Market. I remembered a scarf I had stolen there once, red and silken, one that I would never wear afterward; red was terrible on me. But I recalled running my fingers across it, my eyes flicking up at the stall owner, who stared back, as if he could hear how hard my heart was thumping. *Scusa, signore*… I'd heard Deb say. The owner's eyes left me. Then off I went.

John bought a new leather wallet, and I charged a small and expensive leather purse, feeling that I was paying back some of the old karma. It occurred to me, walking back to the hotel, that the purse was just like the scarf—something I would rarely use, too small to fit all that traveling required, my laptop, for example, or snacks for the children.

At dinner that evening, four of the six tables were set with young kids hosting visiting parents. Some parents watched their kids order drinks for the table with admiration, others looked thirsty for the check. Sitting there, I could have seemed like anyone to those who stared back at me. The thought was pleasing, and for the first time since I'd arrived in Florence earlier that day, I relaxed. I was also alone, John passed out on the bed back at the hotel, requesting a doggie bag for his woes.

The waitress was tending to a table of four American girls next to me, who sat around a table of half-eaten pasta, chests bubbling out of their shirts like the spumante they sipped. Their legs were bare, feet clad with identical army boots, hair and eyes done up. In the low light of the room two of the four faces were illuminated by their screens; one stopped scrolling temporarily to stretch out an arm for a photo, another snapped one of her desiccated plate. The other two were illuminated by their own private conversation, stopping every few minutes to throw their heads back in laughter, whisper, lean into each other. They were clearly the tight ones in the group, with the other two part of the circle but peripherally. Group dynamics were almost too easy to spot. Deb and I had had a few friends like that too. Welcome to join the fun but never invited inside.

I'd met Deb on the first day of orientation, agreed to live with her on the second; by the end of the week we'd moved from the hostel where the students were temporarily housed to our little nest, eighty-eight steps up—how many days did it take before I stopped sleeping in my own room and moved my things into Deb's? The wall between our sleeping quarters had seemed, at the time, superfluous.

Maybe the question I was struggling with now—yes, more wine, I signaled to the waitress—was whether our intimacy during that time wasn't fate bringing two destined souls together but life arbitrarily pairing up two kids on an extended vacation, the kind of uncomplicated setup where it was easy to get along with anyone. The idea of it made me sad, as if most relationships weren't a by-product of circumstance.

The pitch of the girls' laughter scraped against the walls. I didn't have many girlfriends these days. The ones I had were connected to work or to John, with their limits to intimacy. When this had occurred to me recently, I'd tried harder to reach Deb. But Deb had either grown new intimacies with new women or suffered the same problem as me: that work and family were not optimized for female companionship and that once you tried too hard to make something happen—a dinner, a phone call—a friend just became another item on the list of things to maintain. I belched and realized as the waitress took my plate that I had left nothing to bring back to John. I texted to see how he was doing.

Think I have a fever, he responded. *Hungry now.*

It would have been simple to order another plate of pasta to go, but I felt too embarrassed to ask. I thought of texting Deb but resisted the impulse; I didn't want to rub in the fact that I was here without her, eating a nice quiet dinner. Instead I called over the waitress and asked her to send another bottle of spumante to the table of girls from me. "Tell them they remind me of someone," I said. "And to enjoy," I added. I dumped the last of the large carafe in my glass and watched the girls frown at the waitress before slowly looking over at me. I raised my glass at them, suddenly feeling like a horny old man. "Thank you!" the girls sang across the restaurant, then whispered among themselves and began laughing again. A few minutes later they paid their bill and stood, the slats of the chairs stamped against the backs of their thighs. One of them picked up the barely touched bottle and carried it out the door, taking a swig.

Outside the restaurant, I studied the streets with concentration. Again I had drunk too much too fast. Suddenly it had felt like the whole restaurant was staring at me after I sent over the spumante, the odd Don of the back table, and I'd asked for the check. But I still had no food for John. I wandered into a *tabacchi*, but they only sold beer, chocolate, and vacuum-packed bags of peanuts. I turned onto another street and spotted a sign for kebabs, but upon closer inspection the place was closed. I turned another corner and squinted. The American girls were walking in a horizontal line up ahead, passing my bottle from mouth to mouth. I saw them disappear into a building with a neon sign overhead of something that might have been a half-moon, or a taco. I walked up the street and found myself following them inside.

I wasn't sure how to categorize the ambiance. Upscale dive, if that was a thing, with a mix of Italians and exchange students. My stomach was starting to feel sour, but I ordered a sambuca and asked the bartender in Italian if they served food. "Sandwich," he answered, so I added a cold tomato and cheese panino to go. While I waited I looked for the girls and saw half of them at a back table with young men. I strained to see whether the men were Italian or American. The shoes seemed to indicate Italian. I couldn't tell if I wanted to make sure the girls didn't see me or if I secretly hoped they did and invited me over.

"Cheese-a sandwich," the bartender said at some point, sliding a box across the bar.

I paid and realized my bladder was bursting. I followed a sign to the back of the bar, passing the girls' table unnoticed and entered the bathroom, setting John's panino box on the wet sink. For a minute I thought I heard a whimper from the last stall. I paused. Nothing. But when I opened the door to my own stall, I heard it again. I bent down and saw a pair of boots and a pair of sneakers. "Hello?" I called. "Everything all right?" Then I added: "*Tutto bene?*"

Nothing. I was about to head into the stall to pee when I heard another whimper again, louder this time, and thinking of my daughters, I went to the back stall and knocked, then pushed the door in. There were three people in the stall. A girl was pressed against the wall, her dress up, legs wrapped around a man's neck, her face between his legs. The other girl stood there and watched, her cheeks bright red, as if she were the one who was being serviced. As they both turned to look at me, I was startled to realize that it was those same two girls, the close ones, that had been missing from the foursome at the table. The boy was handsome enough, his chin and upper lip glistening under the bad overhead light. Everyone stared at each other for a moment.

Then time fell back on its tracks. One of the girls screamed, and I stumbled out an apology, backing out of the stall to leave without peeing and without the panino. As I threw open the bathroom door, I heard the two girls break into laughter.

"Sick bitch," I heard the other girl say before the door swung closed behind her.

I awoke at Brunelleschi's Palace the next morning with an apocalyptic headache and still-feverish husband. I ordered three cappuccinos under the dead noblemen that oversaw the breakfast room. Their dead eyes appeared judgier than yesterday. I pushed the buffet eggs aside and stared instead into my peach pastry. The image of the night before appeared in the split of the pastry. I missed work. It was easier navigating the id of that world than dealing with the needs and impulses of everything outside it.

It occurred to me that I could no longer remember what desire looked like when I was twenty; I remembered longing for people I hardly knew and I remembered disappointment in the ones I did and I remembered shaving my pussy completely bald because there was so much I felt a girl's body should apologize for back then, or attempt to rectify. Mostly from that time I remembered how it felt to follow Deb around the city like a dog, and how happy it made me, to be given a sense of direction. How much more rewarding that kind of love was. Deb ran the daily and nightly agendas. Deb dressed me from her own closet for each occasion, told me what to order, how to dance, how to smoke. The first time she saw me naked, my pubic area pocked with razor burn, she instructed me never to shave there again, that any man could learn to love some bush. I listened to all of it because I wasn't convinced of my ability to make better decisions. Turning myself over to her in this way provided a primal satisfaction that sex, at that stage in my life, had not yet given me. The only nights that I didn't sleep in her room was when Deb had someone over, the sounds seeping through the wall. I always suggested to my own dates that we went to their place instead of mine. It frightened me, for some reason, to think about how it might feel to do and say things to someone other than Deb that Deb could hear.

I did some emails in the hotel room while John attempted to dress for the day, but after the shower he collapsed back on the bed, and I realized I would be spending the afternoon alone again. I went down to the pharmacy for some aspirin, which I brought back to the room and administered, along with fluids and snacks. I studied him tenderly for a few minutes; it was so easy to love men and children while they slept. I packed his suitcase, leaving an outfit for the flight draped over the chair. I called downstairs and asked about getting an early cab for the morning to the airport. I packed my own suitcase. Then I looked at my watch and realized it was nearly time for the Uffizi tour. I kissed John on the forehead before heading downstairs.

I considered asking for another restaurant recommendation from the hotel as I came down the elevator, but I spotted Deb's doppelgänger again, this time at the hotel bar. The glass of white wine in front of her was perspiring, and the whole mood of the place suddenly seemed cozy, even in its regality. It was the last day of my two-day vacation, and I thought why not roam the Uffizi with a bit of a buzz. I walked over and took a seat at the bar, two stools away.

"I'll have a quick glass of what she's drinking, thanks."

"Verdicchio," said the woman.

"Sorry?"

"The wine."

"Sounds like lettuce," I said, without meaning to be funny but was pleased to see the woman laugh.

"American?"

"Yes."

"Here on business or rich husband?"

I laughed uncomfortably. "I guess I'm the rich husband."

"Ah," said the woman, raising her glass, "good for you."

"And you?"

"Rich husband. Not mine, though. When his wife calls I come down here."

"Oh," I said, suddenly feeling stiff. "I'm sorry."

"Don't be. She knows about me."

We drank quietly for a minute.

"You and your partner aren't open, I take it?"

"Oh, no."

"Ever thought about it?"

"I'm the jealous type."

The woman nodded, to show that she either respected my take or couldn't care less one way or another. It was difficult to tell.

"Last night," I said suddenly, "I walked in on two kids having sex in a bathroom stall."

The woman looked at me with renewed interest. "No kidding."

"There was a third girl in there just watching."

The woman raised her eyebrows and then sipped her drink thoughtfully, as if she were cataloging something for later. Then she said: "Have you ever tried to place a sex spell on someone?"

I coughed into my glass. "To what?"

"A sex spell. To conjure someone you're interested in."

I shook my head.

"It's simple. You think of the person while you're masturbating and then say their name three times while you come."

"Oh."

The woman glanced at the ceiling. "That's how I got Harry."

I laughed harder than I'd remembered laughing in a long time. The only person I wanted to conjure was Deb, and even if I'd tried to sex spell her in an act of desperation, she wouldn't have come and neither would I. We'd kissed once in a bar somewhere near where I currently sat with this stranger, just once after too much tequila, and we never talked about it again. It wasn't surprising to me that women might grapple with the same role-playing complexities in their friendships as they did with the rest of the world, part mother, part mistress. Once when I got my heart broken I remember sitting on a bench and Deb towering above me, her hands stroking my hair, my face pressed against her womb. I remember how safe I felt sleeping in her bed. I remember her farting comfortably under the sheets while she knew I was still awake. I remember her holding my hips and teaching them how to gyrate while we waited in line for the bathroom. I was so happy that year, not because I was young and living a temporary life in a beautiful foreign city, but because I was soaring at the height of female closeness. I'd never felt something like that before with a woman, and once I did, I didn't need much else from life. I didn't care what I wore or what I ate or where I went, so long as I was with Deb. Part of me wondered whether I would have done so well in my career if Deb and I had stayed that close, whether I would have still married John or shot out a couple of kids. Only once I felt her absence did I begin to ask more from life; I began to feel like it owed me something. Now I was here; I was who I was. Someone much different. The woman asked me what I was doing the rest of the day, and I told her my guided museum tour of the Uffizi was just about to start. She didn't actually look anything like Deb up close. We ordered a bottle.

At some point in the day we decided to step out for a cigarette, even though I didn't smoke anymore, and on the other side of the revolving doors I was surprised to run into the evening, the light orange over the city. It wasn't warm, exactly, but it wasn't freezing either, and the crispness felt great. I took the woman down Via Ghibellina, back toward my old place, I pointed up at the top floor, and when I told her I couldn't remember which building it was, the great sadness of the previous day suddenly became ridiculous and we laughed and laughed.

We went into a small trattoria and ordered another bottle. We ordered salads and pastas and meats as if we were fat kings. At a certain point the look of the table sobered me; I became anxious for a reason I couldn't quite name. I could afford everything that sat in front of me, but I had the sudden paranoia that this woman was using me, that she had liquored me up for a free meal. She must have seen all of this cross my face and said, "Don't worry, tonight's Harry's treat," and I felt such relief pour over my body, not because I didn't have to pay but because it felt so nice to be with someone like me, someone like who I was now, who could just splurge on a palace and a meal and not be made to feel like shit about it, and then I wondered if when you got older that was the friendship you looked for, not those who scared you or thrilled you or challenged you but people who mirrored your home life and station, who you could complain to about all the same things and justify choices. When we stumbled back to our hotel I saw there were no missed calls from John and I felt relieved about that too.

I started to walk back to the hotel bar for a nightcap, but the woman grabbed my hand and told me to come upstairs, she wanted me to meet Harry. In the gold door of the elevator I caught our reflections. The image didn't pick up the details of our faces and the effect was startling, like a filter: We looked girlish standing there, photoshopped. We got off on the floor above mine, and it wasn't until I was inside her room, seeing the insides of their suitcases, the smell of a recent shower, that I realized how drunk I was and how weird it was for me to be there. Harry was reading the paper in an armchair by the window, barefoot, and stood to shake my hand, his face neither handsome nor ugly, but nondescript, with stock features for middle age that left no impression, like an ad for medication one scrolled past. I said I needed to be going, and the woman brought me a glass of water, and I found myself sitting down on the bed for a moment to manage drinking it. Harry kissed the woman hello and then kissed her some more. His eyes flicked at me while he did this, but the woman said nothing and did not look at me. The rowdiness of the day suddenly found a shift in register; the room became quiet.

As I sat there on the bed watching them, I wondered if this was how one might interpret revisiting an old self. What seemed to burden me in that moment was not the adulterous couple warming each other up for a fuck. It was not quite the inability to reinhabit old versions of myself—younger, wilder ones, perhaps, which I could only assume was some part of taking this trip—but that I still had to carry all those people with me wherever I went. They always seemed at odds with each other, muddling the true nature of desire while still demanding it find some release. One of them carried Deb, and I missed that version most of all.

I stood to leave. If I hadn't told the woman about the incident in the bathroom stall, would the night still have ended this way? Maybe she thought I'd made it up to suggest this inevitability.

I rode the elevator down one floor and then blundered toward my room, which seemed to be right below the woman and Harry. I struggled to find my key and finally knocked, hoping that John wasn't asleep. He answered the door in the blue flannels he always packed when he traveled. He did not ask me where I had been or why I could barely hold myself steady. He gave me his arms and took me to bed.

I wondered as I lay next to him in the dark if his being there, just right there next to me, was what constituted a certain kind of long-standing love. There would be people in the world who would make you feel like yourself, but what did you call them when they were no longer the ones who carried you through a bad day, a bad trip, who no longer gave you their arms?

I put my head on John's chest and stared at the room's wallpaper, an abstracted depiction of the Florentine fleur-de-lis. The same image everywhere in this city: the center petal closed, erect, while the right and left petals curled back toward the stem. Those two always seemed just moments away from breaking off, like you could blow on them and they'd release.

ITALIAN MIGRANT WORKERS ARE DOING CONSTRUCTION NEXT DOOR

by MARIELLA MEHR

Translated from the German by Caroline Froh

ITALIAN MIGRANT WORKERS ARE doing construction on the Autobahn bridge next door. The smell of hot tar has driven the dogs into their kennels. Our square is empty and gray, except for the yellow car of the postman just passing by the trailers. Because he is afraid of the dogs, he distributes yellow slips in the mailboxes.

You have to go and pick up your package from the local post office. For Mrs. Tonini, this is quite difficult. She is old and her legs refuse to move anymore. So she has to try her daughter, who lives in the trailer next to her, where geraniums are always in bloom. As if they could cope with the gray of the district heating system and the dirty yellow of the communal laundry. Color suffocates here. A mustard flower is blooming out of the top of the gravel pile by the fence. I am ashamed for it. Especially in rainy weather, when even the perpetually wandering cats disappear into the lower part of the trailers. Noldi has fashioned himself a green plastic roof, because it doesn't leak as badly, and roofing felt needs to be replaced every year. It's not like it used to be, when the older Yenish repaired their wagons over the winter. Now we, too, build for eternity. Anything provisional is laughed at.

People don't look forward to summer's arrival anymore; instead we have committed to an eternal winter. The children sing "The Gypsy Life Is Merry" or "I-Don't-Know-What-That-Means."

Even toys are different: domesticity in miniature farmhouse rooms, the inevitable Cadillac. The children come home from school in the afternoons. Standard middle-class fare is cooking on electric stoves. Hedgehogs and dog roasts are mentioned only in secret. Horse meat, too, since horses no longer pull our caravans. This should all be changed, but most people are too tired. Some are counting on the younger generations, but many doubt we'll even be around in the future, maybe as soon as fifty years from now. Will they taxidermy the last Yenish?

Only night knows our sorrow, night and the biting wind over the concrete. In the eyes of the old ones this looks like dying hope. I enjoy talking with them, for their silence speaks of old happinesses—flickering campfires and horses' thudding hooves.

Tiger moved to Switzerland three years ago. He'd been a horse trader in Alsace, and people say he was the best there was. Even a lame horse would hop like a hare if he'd decided to sell it. Tiger and his chewed tobacco pipe and his colorful, rolled-up shirts. Sometimes I hear him talking to the horses he sold, a low, deep song, red wine in his glass. Even his hat is old, his hat that he only ever takes off to scratch his head. He moves so gingerly, it's as if his feet were caressing the earth, the same earth that nourished his horses all those years. As if he knew there would be another going-back one day, which even the gray couldn't prevent.

His dogs howl through the night, as the whores next door keep a lookout for clients and cover up license plates with their barely covered behinds.

—*An excerpt from* Nightmare of the Embryos

THE DECADES

by SUZANNE RHODENBAUGH

THE 1940S

BORN TO A TALL thin brown-eyed aristocrat who became a machinist and an alcoholic, and a petite blue-eyed belle given to histrionics—theirs was a Southern story—I arrived during wartime, near the middle of the century. A neighbor drove my mother to the hospital. My father was off somewhere.

Twice this decade I went missing: as a baby, when I fell off my parents' bed on the wall side and stayed quiet, provoking a frantic neighborhood search. And at five, first grade, when I skipped the school bus and walked home alone "to see if I could do it."

Delicious to remember walking alone, at four or five, through the pine woods to the gazebo my people called a summerhouse, on Aunt Pauline's defunct farm, Zebulon Road, outside Macon, Georgia—we lived there one of the times when we couldn't afford to rent a place. I didn't know we were poor. I was unfettered and unafraid.

THE 1950S

My father died. It was in the spring of first grade. I don't remember much about it. My later conclusion was that my life was enabled—had much more opportunity than my siblings' lives—because my father did die. I didn't have to go through his alcoholic binges, his job losses, the family's frequent moves.

I escaped the turmoil of the family by reading up on the boards that did for a treehouse in the pepper tree out back, on Cayuga Street in Tampa. There I entered multitudinous biographies that showed what a person could be and do beyond their natural-born limits. And the Walter Farley books: the power and beauty of the horse.

Fears manifested. One by Farmer's Field, those wild acres bordering the school playground—nothing bad ever happened but there was danger there; and from the man who cleaned his gun on his porch after supper; and from the Doberman other neighbors let out after dark, whose nose came to my waist. And fear, after so many warnings, when crossing busy streets; and fear I would never be pretty; and fear from the true stories told: our neighbor Mr. Brown put dynamite caps in his mouth at work and blew his head off; and vague fear at the McNabs'. They came from Honduras, a foreign place. I was at their house a lot, but the smells seemed alien. And the great-uncle who couldn't make a sound—because his wife talked so much, my mother said. And fear the day I was ironing alone and the iron started popping and sending off sparks, whereby I ran all the way to my friend Mary Lou's, whose mother came and put the fire out.

And then the humiliations. The time the teacher wouldn't let me go to the bathroom, so I peed my pants and hoped no one would see the trickle running between the desks. But of course they did and laughed, especially the boys, and when I told my mother what happened she made a big uproar at the school and I was put in another class, which made things worse. And how the boys made fun of my violin case, so that I left off playing and lost the beginning of that knowledge.

THE 1960s

The formative fateful decade: everything happened! To me and to my world. When I was a junior in high school, I skipped school the first and only time of my life to take a bus downtown to hear Jack Kennedy, who was running for President that fall of 1960. I stood just a few feet from him, in those days before assassinations and mass shootings.

I graduated from high school, went to college, got married at nineteen, divorced at twenty-two. After college I worked for a year as a bibliographer in the university's library and made a big fool of myself earnestly promising the head of the library that I'd keep on the lookout for a Gutenberg Bible. He told me to—a joke I didn't get.

I had a baby out of wedlock and gave her up for adoption and moved to Atlanta to work for the War on Poverty, the Office of Economic Opportunity's Southeast Regional Office, the most intense work experience of my life. I was a field representative in the Florida Division of the Community Action Program, determining annual grants to community action agencies in the Fort Lauderdale, Sarasota, Gainesville, Pensacola and Northeast Florida regions, and Head Start grants to others, especially the trouble-ridden one in the Fort Myers area, and to the State of Florida poverty program in the governor's office. I enforced civil rights compliance, gave or arranged technical assistance, and trained VISTA volunteers. OEO was where I worked and virtually lived, all social contacts issuing out of it as well.

I walked in Martin Luther King's funeral march and stood outside the church with the thousands of others and listened to the funeral over loudspeakers and saw two celebrities act unpardonably: Richard Nixon and James Brown, both coming in convertibles, from which they enthusiastically waved at the crowd, as if it were a political rally or a rock concert. I saw Bobby Kennedy, the last politician in my whole life I would completely believe in, quietly enter the church with Ethel. He would be killed within two months.

In 1969 I went to do farmwork and study Hebrew on an Israeli kibbutz "to get out of the rat race," as the ad in *New Republic* had promised, and after a few months flew home on a DC-3 piloted by a friend of mine and John Hawke, who flew the filming plane for the movie *Battle of Britain*. Over New York City they let me have the controls, and I didn't even have a driver's license.

Then during a protest march in DC over the Vietnam War, I got hired by Gerson Green, who'd been head of research and development for OEO, to come be his assistant at University Research Corporation, which didn't have anything to do with a university and didn't really do research, and laid me off a few months in when they lost some contracts and grants, and I'd just moved to DC for the job. After which I worked for a temporary employment agency, going out on mainly clerical assignments.

At a demonstration in support of the Chicago Seven I got arrested, was thrown in the back of a paddy wagon and taken to jail, but "movement people" were already at the jail and got me and hundreds of others out.

Though the sixties didn't truly happen until the early seventies, during the 1960s my world got much larger, and I was able to put aside the hurt of putting my daughter up for adoption. I'd not yet calculated the costs to my child, and to my own soul.

THE 1970S

The decade I turned thirty had great highs and lows for me, and I attained a measure of maturity. But first, after the kibbutz caper, I spent a winter working as a waitress and chambermaid in a Vermont ski lodge. It seemed like a good idea at the time (so many things did!) and was great fun, though I never learned to ski.

Then my life began to sound like a résumé, which it started out being. After Vermont I worked in DC for the preposterously named Institute for the Study of Health and Society, where I wrote a guidebook for training consumers and community groups on how they might affect the health care system and edited a book of readings on such, and there got the idea to go to graduate school in public health, so that my wish to help the poor might be accompanied by some actual knowledge. I got a US Public Health Service Traineeship to study for a master's of public health in medical care administration at University of Michigan, where I spent the fall of 1972 through the spring of 1974. That 1973 summer I went for an administrative residency to Bellaire, Ohio, to a clinic system that served coal-mining families, poor people and others in the surrounding small towns and rural areas of eastern Ohio and the West Virginia panhandle. (It was poet James Wright's country, but I wouldn't know that for years.)

In Bellaire I met George Goldstein, the clinic system director, and his wife Lois, who became lifelong influences on me, friends, and virtual parents. There I also entered wholeheartedly into the world of coal miners, their union and history, and their health care.

After graduation I took a job in Johnstown, Pennsylvania, as the assistant to the regional administrator of the United

Mine Workers of America Health and Retirement Fund, the third-party payer, ombudsman and facilities' initiator for mining families' health care and pensions.

I carved out my own role: determining admittance to participation of physicians and clinics in a ten-county area and making initial financial arrangements; trying to organize new clinics in outlying areas; overseeing the first program-determined budget for the region; and generally writing the region's responses to a range of major changes in the Fund being generated out of the DC headquarters. I tried to stave the bleeding from the move to computerization, a disastrous tail-wagging-the-dog enterprise, which so screwed up service to beneficiaries that it helped bring down the Fund's thirty-year existence in the 1978 contract negotiations between the Union and the Bituminous Coal Operators Association.

In mid-1976 I met Tom, who would be my husband. I fell in love, first, with the sound of his voice, as I arranged for him to come to Pennsylvania to interview for a new clinic's directorship. December of that year we married, and I moved to DC, where he was assistant to the president of the Union. We felt his kids, his seven-year-old daughter and especially his adopted six-year-old Black son, would do better in DC than in rural Pennsylvania.

I went hip deep into the new role of full-time stepmother; I felt the kids had been jacked around too much already to babysitters and day care centers, and wanted to do the best I could. I didn't think I could meet my own standards as a full-time worker, wife and mother, and felt I should give up the work outside the house.

We bought a house in Takoma Park, Maryland, in a neighborhood that included a lot of mixed-race families and immigrants. One month after moving in, a man came into the house, where I was sewing alone, grabbed me from behind, hooded and raped me, then tied me up and left me in a closet.

To cope, I got very involved in trying to organize the neighborhood and town to catch the rapist and to reduce crime in general. This work led to years of organizing, mainly through a new neighborhood organization, on issues of schools, crime, voter registration, zoning and code enforcement, town and school board elections.

More than any time before or after, I felt a sense of community, of helping out and being helped by neighbors who became good friends. My husband and I were enjoying the kids, working on the house, having a lot of fun at neighborhood events and parties. It was the happiest time of my life. One of its enrichments was going to Alaska in 1979, accompanying Tom for his work. We took bush planes to remote villages, went whitewater rafting, hiked at Mt. McKinley, took a ship up Glacier Bay.

I was also writing more and beginning to publish more. I had a rich, full life. The problems with our son in school—the refusal to cooperate, to do homework, to try at anything in a sustained way—were ongoing, but I was not yet defeated.

THE 1980s

In 1980 Ronald Reagan was elected President. In the future some would wax nostalgic about him, but his campaigns and presidency were really the beginning of the hate-government period, which seems never to end. The country had Nixon and Watergate in the 1970s and now had a President who was a real-life third-rate version of a President from the movies, a cliché and a fool.

Tom directed a non-profit that gave technical assistance to economic development projects in poor communities. It was completely federally funded. We knew it probably had an unlikely future but didn't know how soon. Early 1981 found Tom jobless and both of us facing a daunting job market in the DC area, where thousands of highly qualified people had lost their jobs from either government cutbacks or defunding in the nonprofit sector.

I had been out of the job market only a few years but found myself being interviewed—when I could get an interview for a health care job—as if I had been in a cave or a coma.

The family survived on Tom's short-term consulting jobs, and my occasional health-care-related consulting assignments, but it was a dicey, high-stress time. As the children entered their teenage years, the stress grew exponentially. Our son, who was off-the-charts brilliant, failed a grade. Then I was hospitalized when I was briefly feared to have throat cancer.

The closing of the kids' school was also in the works, due to a countywide plan to artificially increase integration by closing one of the few schools, Takoma Park Junior High, that was naturally integrated because of the community it drew from. They wanted to bus our kids to predominantly white schools.

Four other women and I spearheaded Save Our Community School, raising $10,000 from bake sales and the like, getting the (dubious) pro bono assistance of Covington & Burling, a prestigious DC law firm, writing letters to the editor and letters to the school board, and generally raising hell, including closing down a secret late-night school board meeting by marching in with a crowd singing "We Shall Not Be Moved."

The school was saved, but the family was not. The kids chose, after counseling, to go live with their mother in Massachusetts, starting at the end of a school year. Tom meanwhile had gotten a job in Connecticut and been spending four days a week there and three in Takoma Park.

The fall of 1984 I won a seat in a competitively entered poetry workshop at George Washington University taught by visiting writer Julia Alvarez, who urged me to get a master of fine arts in writing and try to get a book published.

In October 1984 I moved to Connecticut. I had lost the kids, my neighborhood and town, and my writing community. I turned forty. I applied for the MFA program at Vermont College, requiring residency only two weeks twice a year. I had decided to stop feeling like a failure by going full tilt at the writing I'd been doing since undergraduate school.

In January 1985 I entered the two and a half years I'd spend working on that MFA: a new world. A lot of it was phony and pathetic. A lot of it was beautiful and intense. I read 125 books, wrote many new poems, wrote an ambitious critical thesis on about twenty-five modern poets on a "spectrum of relation" to a figure of suffering, using Martin Buber's *I and Thou* as my framework.

I began to teach part-time as an adjunct at several colleges, and in the Johns Hopkins University writing-by-mail program for highly gifted students in grades 8–12. I went to the Bread Loaf Writers' Conference as the Farrar Scholar in Poetry in 1988 and studied there with Philip Levine. My first poetry chapbook came out in 1989. I had several well-received readings in New York, including one where I was one of three finalists for the Barnard New Women Poets Prize for a full-length book. I lost, as I would for sixteen and a half years in poetry book competitions, for which I was a finalist about thirty-five times. I got discouraged, but Tom's support for my writing was unfailing, and I am naturally virtually irrepressible.

In 1989 I began my first attempts to find my birthdaughter, who was now of age. A Tampa lawyer lied to me about the girl's situation, and I didn't question or complain when I found out because the shame and grief were too much.

That same year I fell on icy steps and sprained both my shoulders. I also began an early menopause.

My mother had not countenanced "falling apart" or "breaking down" and I attended to those values, maybe out of strength, maybe out of not being able to fully acknowledge failure as a mother, as a stepmother, as a writer, as a co-provider by employment. And also because of the joy the writing gave me: it wouldn't let me alone.

THE 1990S

In the fall of 1990 Tom and I moved to Richmond, Virginia, for his new job. I didn't dread the move because I would be closer to friends in Takoma Park and DC, and felt homeward bound in the sense of returning to the South.

An antique dealer told me Richmond wasn't nostalgic for antebellum days, but missed, rather, the eighteenth century. I found it an easy place to live, but its unfriendliness a near-impossible nut to crack. I tried to get adjunct teaching and couldn't. I tried to get involved in the "neighborhood" organization—a very large, top-down association where you couldn't even ask a question without being granted permission; and I tried to understand local politics, which were as closed-off as everything else about Richmond.

Being a Southerner there was irrelevant too, unless you'd been in Richmond three hundred years. The few friendly people I met were from other places, or other parts of Virginia, particularly the mountains.

But it was a good place to get a lot of writing done, and I did, now essays as well as poetry. I had two more chapbooks published, and pushed on with the effort to get a full-length poetry book published.

In 1993 I was a Poetry Fellow at the Vermont Studio Center, studying briefly with Diane Wakoski, who deemed everyone to have "one story" (except herself). There I got the idea to imagine poems starting from different locations in the house in Tampa where I'd lived the longest during my growing up, and out of this wrote a large batch of strong new poems.

One year I was the writer-in-residence for a suburban school system, teaching writing to kids in grades 6–12. My introduction to the book of their writing, in which I said writing talent was fairly common but commitment less so—and praised particular students who had worked hard and consistently—was censored by the school system, due to the "everyone is equal" philosophy prevailing then (and still), etc. Some of the students' writing, particularly the humorous parts, was censored as well.

In 1994 Tom gave me a surprise fiftieth birthday party in a rowhouse inn, one of several where Edgar Allan Poe had played during part of his childhood. The party was stupendously satisfying: friends came from many parts of my life, and those who couldn't come sent letters, cards, recordings. The weekend following, the party continued.

1994 was also the beginning of resuming my search for my birthdaughter. I wrote letters, made calls; connected with search groups of birthparents, adoptees and adoptive parents; registered with state and international adoption registries. I also tried a few deceptive and/or illegal means, such as pretending to be a researcher on the health status of young women born the early fall of 1967 in Tampa, Florida.

At the same time, I was researching and writing what was eventually a sixty-five-page genre-challenged piece on my genealogy, which I could trace to 1290 in the village of Checkendon, in Oxfordshire, England, this narrative punctuated by historical happenings of national or international significance. I hoped to give this to my daughter if I found her.

By late 1996 I had taken every tack I'd known to do, and failed, and hired a private detective. By early 1997 he'd found three families he thought were likely possibilities. I intuited the correct one, and spoke by phone at length with the adoptive mother, who was kind but said her daughter—named Suzanne—had never had any interest in knowing, or knowing of, her birthparents.

With help from a professional searcher, I found my daughter and called. She hung up on me, as she would a couple days later, and the few times in subsequent years I tried again.

That was a catastrophic maw, a giant hole in my universe, and not fixable. I had at least learned my daughter—now almost thirty—had seemingly had a good life, was well, had graduated from college, married, and had a child. My nightmares about her ceased. It felt like another failure hung on my neck, but it was of my own making and I had to live with it.

While the search was still ongoing, the fall of 1995 Tom and I went to England on an itinerary determined by a combination of my genealogy, and English writers I loved. This trip was a complete joy: to go through the homes of Thomas Hardy and Jane Austen, to sit on the moor where Charlotte Brontë walked, to visit the Poets' Corner in Westminster

Abbey. And to see Hardy's pet cemetery with its tiny headstones, and the sign on the front of the house saying in Latin, "What of the night?"

In 1996 my idol and father figure George Goldstein died. At his memorial service in Pittsburgh, I read an elegy to him: "Good Night, Sweet Prince."

By the end of the decade Tom and I were on the move again, this time to St. Louis. I knew that city was in the middle of the country, somewhere, and that Chuck Berry lived there, but little more. In March 1999 we moved into a brick Victorian house in south St. Louis, across the street from the huge and gorgeous Tower Grove Park. We almost immediately got involved in the neighborhood association, and I led a move to prevent our alderwoman from having a median built down the middle of our street, which was used by emergency vehicles and was also an evacuation route. In a neighborhood-sponsored debate, I strongly bested the alderwoman, who had tried some heavy-handed tactics to intimidate me, such as stationing a police car beside our house.

We also quickly got to know neighbors, who initiated a weekly Chicken Night at a local pub—huge fried-chicken dinners cooked by a Serbian biker, $3.99 complete; and soon, a softball team, The Drumsticks. I didn't play but Tom did, though he was about twenty years older than most of the team, which constituted a frequently inept but extremely well-educated bunch, including a classics professor, a couple of architects, lawyers, a performance artist, a research physician, a sculptor, an art museum curator, etc. I was the team's poet laureate: an excellent position which entailed no duties whatsoever.

2000–2009

These years, the decade I turned sixty, were outturning again—to a neighborhood, a city, new writing friends. At first St. Louis felt like a re-experience of the Takoma Park days, though I'd eventually feel they weren't as spirited or as effective, but certainly earthier and more feisty than the days in Richmond.

Losses came too of course. In 2000 my friend and public-health mentor Avedis Donabedian died; and my best friend Aimee Gibson. Aimee and I had been coworkers at OEO in Atlanta and in the ski lodge in Vermont, and roommates in DC. Aimee had been "person of honor" at my wedding. I had gone through Aimee's long decline from severe multiple sclerosis.

In 2002 my mother died, the pain of which took me by surprise and lasted about five years. In 2004 my eldest sister Peggy died.

I had cataract surgery on both eyes and got my first effective treatment for chronic ankle sprains and foot pain.

In 2000, at age fifty-six, I finally won a national poetry book competition for *Lick of Sense*, chosen by Alicia Ostriker for the Marianne Moore Poetry Prize from Helicon Nine Editions. That press, based in Kansas City, in 2001 gave me a reading there, and a warm welcoming party afterwards at the home of poet and publisher Gloria Vando and her husband Bill Hickok. In 2001 I had another chapbook published as well, and taught creative writing one semester at Webster University in 2002. For a time I was assistant editor at the literary magazine *River Styx*; writing "Arts in the 'Hood" features for the neighborhood newsletter; and writing book reviews for the *St. Louis Post-Dispatch* and *Kansas City Star.*

These years I was building gardens in my front and back yards, and doing a declining amount of neighborhood and political involvement. In 2008 I tried registering voters by going door to door for the Obama campaign, found it ineffective, and set up a voter-registration table in my front yard, at a busy corner, where I held sway late afternoons several days a week, figuring people coming home from work who wanted to register but hadn't found the time yet could easily register. This worked well, and I never forgot the man in his seventies who couldn't read or write, but whose niece brought him there to register by signing his X, so he could vote for Obama; and the woman whose husband was under a restraining order and who, she was afraid, would find her if she registered, which worry I got resolved with the Board of Elections.

In 2006 Tom, who was now consulting or working part-time, did a study of the Moscow School of Political Studies and recommended a long-range plan. Thus began a new international focus for him, and on the sidelines my involvement as well.

The School, founded in the early 1990s by Russian dissidents Lena Nemirovskaya and Yuri Senotsov, began around their kitchen table around the time of the overturn of Communism. It evolved into a series of short-term seminars for activists, journalists, academics, lawyers, non-governmental organization workers and others on how democracy works, with speakers from Europe, the US, Russia and some of the former satellite countries. In time a follow-up seminar was developed, with delegates coming to the US for seminars in either St. Louis and Washington, DC, or Chicago and DC. Tom administered the US programs.

The School took over a big chunk of our hearts. Lena is a charismatic international figure whose clear-eyed unremitting commitment to democracy, which Russia has never had in its thousand-year history, draws in anyone who speaks with her past ten minutes. She leaves people wanting to know how they can help.

My help consisted of little more than having dinners at home for small groups of seminar delegates when they were in St. Louis. But it was a new dimension: meeting people who wanted to change their country, with the stakes and risks extremely high.

2010–2019

This decade was life-changing for my country, and for me. In September 2013 Tom had a heart attack. He survived, but with some initial complications and the fear another attack might happen. Sometimes I slept in my clothes in anticipation of having to drive him to the hospital in an emergency, and the next spring I had to be hospitalized briefly for extreme high blood pressure. Sometimes too I had episodes of vertigo.

This decade when I turned seventy is also when Tom and I took on helping our grandson, David, who came to live with us in 2019. David had had a chaotic upbringing with a volatile, now drug-using mother, and a largely absent father, our now alcoholic son. We had had to have the help of a private detective to find him and his mother, who didn't want her son to have any contact with anyone related to the boy's father. We wanted David to be able to use the college funds we had been invested in since the boy's birth. We had seen him only three or four times while he was growing up.

David arrived with a suitcase that might serve for a weekend—all his belongings—and no winter coat. In the ensuing months and years we got him new glasses, medical, dental and mental health care, clothes, a computer, a phone, driving lessons, enrollment in a nearby community college, and help with getting a part-time job. We eventually got him a car that he participated in paying for.

We learned he had dropped out of school in the ninth or tenth grade—he couldn't remember—and spent the years until age twenty-two on a computer in his room, his online friends his only ones. At our house he had to learn basically everything of the day-to-day, as well as social interaction. Fortunately, David is kind, gentle, extremely intelligent, and has no habits with drugs, alcohol or violence.

A month and a half after he started community college, the pandemic shut everything down. He continued working part-time and continued his courses online, but saw, as we did, how lacking that experience was compared to in-person education.

The decade had begun for me with publication by WordTech of my second full-length poetry book, *The Whole Shebang*. In 2011 I began a correspondence with a teacher in Vladimir, Russia, one I'd met at a US seminar, who had her students translate some of my short poems into Russian and make an illustrated booklet of them. In 2012 I self-published *Sarah's Civil War: The Edited Diary, 1859–1865, of Sarah Lois Wadley*, in an edition of about fifty copies, largely for family. I had learned of the diary by my great-great-aunt from a nephew who found it online.

In the spring of 2013 Tom and I went to Russia, where he'd been three times previously. To prepare I read *War and Peace*. I'd been reading Russian history and literature for several years, trying to understand. We went first to St. Petersburg, where I got food poisoning that kept me in a hotel room most of the first week, but where I was able to see Dostoyevsky's apartment; then took a train to Moscow. There we saw Mayakovsky's room, and the new Jewish museum, and took a side trip to Chekhov's home in Melikhovo. But mainly we'd come for a Moscow School of Political Studies seminar in Golitsnyo, that year a session themed "Literature and Power." I spoke on a panel chaired by English actor Ralph Fiennes on Shakespeare's *Coriolanus*, which as a film he had directed and starred in.

At the beginning of 2016 Tom and I went to Fort Myers, where my sister Katherine was in hospice and died. That year we also went to Oxford, England, for a seminar for Russian journalists.

That was also, of course, a momentous presidential election year. I was the female Hillary Clinton delegate from my ward, and attended the convention to elect St. Louis delegates to the state convention, one of twenty-three women who gave short speeches prior to the voting. When Clinton staff members advised the crowd how to vote, I stood up and objected, which encouraged others to object, after which the staff members ceased condescending.

Election night 2016 Tom and I were in DC for a Moscow School seminar. He'd arranged for the Russian delegates to watch the election returns at a restaurant. I left early for our hotel, a little puzzled at how Donald Trump seemed to be ahead but convinced the next morning would bring news of Clinton's win. The next morning's news caused the Russian delegates to say, "Well, at least you have real elections—we know before the voting who will win." Before I even saw the Russian group, I met a maid in the hotel corridor, an Iraqi immigrant who'd been in the US eighteen years, and who hugged me and said, "All we want is to work and have a better life." The woman was afraid under Trump she'd be deported, and was crying.

After the election I felt an urgent need to Do Something, to make something better. I attended a YMCA session on teaching children to read, and was so put off by the inanity of it—the "teacher" throwing candy to the adult audience when someone gave a correct answer—that I quit.

In 2017 my brother Bill died. Now my parents and all my siblings were gone. Maybe unconsciously because of that, and because I felt neither of my stepchildren nor any of my nieces and nephews would care about my writing at my death, should Tom die before I, that year I made an arrangement with the special collections division of the University of South Florida Library to house my literary papers. Though I suspected the willingness there was largely simply because I was one of USF's earliest graduates, I was grateful. I hoped someday some Ph.D. student, desperate for a thesis topic, would happen on the collection and write about it, and the world would know of my poetry. (A friend had once said to me, "You made an unfortunate career choice: you'll have to die to succeed.")

Also in 2017 I self-published an essay collection, *The Deepest South I've Gotten*, short essays on people, places, politics and poetry. I had tried several years to get it published and been told sometimes that only the personal essays should be included or, alternately, only the literary ones, or etc., and concluded that there was no outlet for a collection that was all these things, plus humorous in spots.

2020–

The spring of 2020, the first full year of the pandemic, I was hit by a car while crossing with the walk signal, with the light, a block from my house. I had put out my arms, as if to stop the car. Fortunately, the car was going slowly.

I had bruises up and down my left side, I would learn, but was more worried about the pandemic than injuries and avoided going to the hospital. For reasons I was never able to determine, the driver didn't get even a ticket.

In 2021, the year he turned eighty, Tom was diagnosed with bladder cancer. He had surgery followed by three years of treatment, and continued the gym workouts and walking he'd been doing since his heart attack.

That year Homestead Lighthouse Press, run by Robert McDowell, the poet, editor, novelist and critic, and former long-time co-editor of Story Line Press and the magazine *The Reaper*, accepted my third full-length poetry book, *The Girl Who Quit at Leviticus*. It was published the next year. This was joy indeed after such a long wait. Publication of my first book hadn't made the second any easier, nor the second any easier for the third.

2022 was also the year our grandson David moved into his own apartment and got a good job at a large hospital complex and its satellite hospitals and clinics, setting up or fixing computer systems.

In 2023 I was diagnosed with skin cancer, and early the next year had five and a half hours of Mohs surgery on my face and neck.

The fall of 2024 Tom and I went to British Columbia, and I did the kind of thing I do only if Tom or some friend goads me into doing: going out on a glacier, for example.

We gave a fundraiser for Elad Gross, the Democratic candidate for Missouri attorney general. He lost. And that fall the unthinkable happened: Donald Trump was reelected, which rendered me virtually silent.

In December, impossibly, I turned eighty.

I'm still the girl who was a majorette in junior high, who won jitterbug contests in high school, who hitchhiked alone at night from the ski lodge where I worked in Vermont to New York City to see a guy I was crazy about, who raised hell and had a lot of fun and suffered in many ways, as almost everyone does, and got back up, and who wrote it all down.

CONTRIBUTORS

KHARI DAWSON is a multigenre writer based in the Washington, DC, area. She earned a BA in English from the University of San Francisco in 2024. Her work has been featured in *Poetry* magazine and on the *Cult. Magazine* website. She is a fellow of the Watering Hole Poetry Organization.

MICHAEL DEFORGE draws comics and posters in Toronto. His most recent book was *Holy Lacrimony*. "Universal Studios Monsters" is excerpted from his forthcoming short story collection *All the Cameras In My Room*.

KATY DERBYSHIRE is the translator of a number of contemporary German writers, including Inka Parei, Heike Geissler, Olga Grjasnowa, Annett Gröschner, and Christa Wolf. Her translation of Clemens Meyer's *Bricks and Mortar* won the 2018 Straelen Translation Prize. She is the cohost of a monthly translation lab and the bimonthly *Dead Ladies Show*.

PERCIVAL EVERETT is the author of more than thirty books of fiction and poetry, including the novel *James*, which won the Pulitzer Prize and the National Book Award. Everett's paintings have been exhibited in Los Angeles and internationally. From June to October 2025 he had a solo exhibition at CARLOCINQUE Gallery in Milan in collaboration with Show Gallery. The paintings published here are from his 2024 solo show, *Redaction*, which was exhibited at Show

Gallery in Los Angeles. The text accompanying this portfolio is a lightly edited excerpt from a conversation between J. C. Gabel and Everett published by Hat & Beard Press in the companion monograph. Artwork courtesy of Show Gallery.

CAROLINE FROH is the translator of Milena Michiko Flašar's novel *Mr. Katō Plays Family* and a collection of prose by Mariella Mehr entitled *Nightmare of the Embryos*, which is forthcoming from New Directions. Caroline lives and works in the mountains of northern New Mexico.

SIMON HAN is the author of the novel *Nights When Nothing Happened.* He teaches creative writing at Tufts University.

JUDITH HERMANN was born in Berlin in 1970. She is the author of several novels and story collections, including *Alice*, which was short-listed for the Independent Foreign Fiction Prize; *Where Love Begins*; and *Summerhouse, Later*, which won the Kleist Prize. Her novel *Daheim* was a best seller and won the Rheingau and the Bremen Literature Prizes. Her work has been translated into thirty-five languages, and a number of her short stories have been adapted for film. She lives and works in Berlin.

KEVIN JOHNSTON is a writer and documentary producer. Based in Los Angeles, born and raised in New York, he's currently at work on a collection of short stories. Ask him about his dog.

SUSANNA KWAN is the author of *Awake in the Floating City*. She lives in San Francisco and teaches writing with The Dream Side.

ASHLEY NELSON LEVY is the author of the novel *Immediate Family*. In 2015, she cofounded Transit Books, an independent publishing house with a focus on international literature.

SEAN LEWIS is a freelance illustrator of picture books and a designer for animation. His books include *I'll Get to the Bottom of This!* (A24) by Daniel Kwan and *Earth's Incredible Places, Grand Canyon* (Flying Eye Books) and he has two forthcoming books about the moon (Tundra Books) and a ghost (Simon and Schuster). He art directed the stop motion animated music video for Fleet Foxes, *Featherweight*. Sean lives in Toronto, Canada.

MARIELLA MEHR (1947–2022) worked as a journalist and became a unique prose artist, noted for the quietly overpowering style of her fiction, her somewhat unclassifiable essays, and her five novels. She was the recipient of numerous prizes, including the Prize of the Swiss Schiller Foundation (1996), the ProLitteris Prize (2012), the Literary Prize of the canton of Graubünden (2016), and a Recognition Prize of the city of Zürich for her body of work (2017).

SAM MUNSON is the author of *The Sofa* (Two Dollar Radio), *Dog Symphony* (New Directions), *The War Against the Assholes*

(Saga), and *The November Criminals* (Doubleday). His fiction has appeared in *The Baffler*, *Granta*, *Guernica*, *McSweeney's Quarterly*, *n+1*, *Tablet*, and elsewhere. He is the cofounder of *The New York Review of Dreams* (www.rateyourdream.com).

CATHERINE NIU's stories and essays have appeared or are forthcoming in *The Cincinnati Review*, *Best Small Fictions 2025*, *AGNI*, *The Iowa Review*, *Alaska Quarterly Review*, *Michigan Quarterly Review*, *The Gettysburg Review*, and elsewhere. She lives in Houston, where she is an Inprint Fondren Foundation fellow and fiction editor at *Gulf Coast*.

KATIE PETERSON is the author of some books of poetry, including *Fog and Smoke* and *Life in a Field*. She teaches in the creative writing program at UC Davis and lives in Berkeley, California, with her husband, the photographer Young Suh, and their daughter Emily. She is working on a book about the poet Gerard Manley Hopkins and the idea of progress, a truly absurd idea, if you think about it.

SUZANNE RHODENBAUGH is the author of the poetry books *The Girl Who Quit at Leviticus* (Homestead Lighthouse Press, 2022), *The Whole Shebang* (WordTech, 2010), and *Lick of Sense* (Helicon Nine Editions, 2001); four chapbooks; and the essay collection *The Deepest South I've Gotten* (Hell Yes Press, 2017). She edited *Sarah's Civil War: The Edited Diary, 1859–1865, of Sarah Lois Wadley* (Bluebird, 2012). She lives in St. Louis. Her favorite word, for both sound and sense, is *gone*.

MEARA SHARMA is a writer, artist, and editor of *Elastic*, a magazine of psychedelic art. She lives in London and Glasgow.

SHRUTI SWAMY is the author of the story collection *A House Is a Body*, and a novel, *The Archer*. She lives in San Francisco.

WALKER TATE is a cartoonist and illustrator living in New York. His comic *Laser Eye Surgery* was published by Fantagraphics Underground in August. More of his work can be found at varietypak.net and walkertate.com.

EMILY GRAY TEDROWE is the author of three novels, most recently *The Talented Miss Farwell* (HarperCollins, 2020). She lives in Chicago.

SOUVANKHAM THAMMAVONGSA's stories have appeared in *The New Yorker*, *The Paris Review*, *The Atlantic*, *Harper's Magazine*, and *Granta*.

ADAM WILSON is the author of four books including the forthcoming novel, *Fail Sons*. He is a National Jewish Book Award finalist and a recipient of the *Paris Review*'s Terry Southern Prize, and his fiction, essays, and criticism have appeared in *Harper's*, *The New Yorker*, *Tin House*, and *The Best American Short Stories*, among many other publications. He teaches at Columbia University and lives in Brooklyn with his wife and their two sons.

McSWEENEY'S 75
guest-edited by Eli Horowitz

Guest-edited by longtime McSweeney's editor Eli Horowitz, our seventy-fifth issue contains ten radiant stories, each published as an individual booklet with stunning art by ten different artists. All ten booklets are collected inside a beautiful and sturdy and elaborately foil-stamped dossier-like case, which opens (rather extravagantly) to reveal a series of accordion pockets—each one containing a pair of booklets—and snaps shut (rather satisfyingly) with a magnetic closure. In these brilliant literary debuts there are fish guts, meteor hunters, military coups, ghost towns, and fake orphans. The stories, whose authors and settings span continents, dazzle in their originality of vision and voice. They announce themselves with bravado, excellence, and energy.

McSWEENEY'S 76: AFTERSHOCKS
guest-edited by Alia Malek

McSweeney's 76: Aftershocks presents a collection of contemporary Syrian prose—short stories, novel excerpts, and plays—that chronicles the literal and metaphorical earthquakes that haunt the Syrian people. Guest-edited by acclaimed Syrian American journalist Alia Malek, and encompassing the work of eight Arabic translators and sixteen Syrian writers (some of which have never before been translated in English), these contributors write across diasporic and refugee experiences, as well as from inside present-day Syria. In these pages, skeletons fall in love, Damascus alleys become time portals, minarets gush blood, and photographs become more human than humans. These stories ask us to imagine the unimaginable. They ask not "what is real?" but rather "how can this be real?"

McSWEENEY'S 77

Three-time National Magazine Award–winning *McSweeney's Quarterly* returns, now helmed by new Editor Rita Bullwinkel. Inside this ecstatic paperback you'll find a stunningly exuberant and delirious portfolio of paintings by former *Quarterly* Editor Claire Boyle, and new work by seventeen writers. Gasp in awe at a story by Mieko Kawakami told entirely through the lens of overheard phone calls; a sci-fi epic by Yuri Herrera; fresh, heart-stopping, and scathingly beautiful prose by Venita Blackburn, Joanna Howard, and Icarus Koh—a never-before-published fiction writer; and brilliant letters from Nell Zink, Jennifer S. Cheng, Elisa Gonzalez, and more! Get through the winter blues with this issue's vibrating, radiant, maximalist energy and stand squarely in opposition to the literary vogue du jour of cold, minimalist austerity.

McSWEENEY'S 78

guest-edited by Thi Bui and Vu Tran

In *McSweeney's 78: The Make Believers*, ten writers of the Vietnamese diaspora write from the eclectic hodgepodge that is their shared imagination of what it means to be "Vietnamese." Packaged in a beautiful foil-stamped cigar box (with art by Bui on each and every surface), and including two booklets, one menu, and a glossary of broken Vietnamese, the work in this issue spans from highbrow to lowbrow, proper to naughty, logical to absurd, and painful to funny. Published on the occasion of the fiftieth anniversary of the end of the Vietnam War, its contributors work across perspectives and multiple languages. In this completely singular, nothing-else-of-its-kind anthology, these artists write (and illustrate!) from a place of collective loss and joy.

McSWEENEY'S 79

Coming to you at the intersection of book and tapestry, the seventy-ninth issue of our National Magazine Award–winning *Quarterly* is embroidered from head to toe—using precisely 133,095 stitches of thread—with the art of Marta Monteiro. Inside this tactile, textile, tangerine-backdropped, cloth-bound art object are ten new stories, two fresh novel excerpts, six timely letters, an essay as sharp as a blade, a stunningly surreal slice of a graphic novel by Patrick Keck, and a shockingly beautiful, hot-pink suite of Mary Magdalenes painted by Leanne Shapton. As your fingers caress the raised topography of this issue's beyond-belief weave, marvel at a novel excerpt by Helen DeWitt and Ilya Gridneff in which invented languages make a play; a story by Ahmed Naji that circles Cairo rap clashes; a captivating, climate-terror portrait of a story by T. C. Boyle; three totally crisp, sentence-gem-adorned stories by Diane Williams; dazzling letters by Jac Jemc, Meng Jin, Rebekah Bergman, and so much more!

McSWEENEY'S 80

Clipped into the three metal rings of this school-binder-inspired issue are no less than seven (!) individual book art objects, including: a forty-eight-page grid-ruled sketchbook by Eisner winner Adrian Tomine; an accordion-shaped flower catalog by Pulitzer Prize finalist Yiyun Li; an end-of-the-world Scantron questionnaire by Pip Adam; a crossword about being in (and out of) love by Chris Ames; and an acrylic stencil by Tamara Shopsin. All this plus new work from Lucy Corin, Brittany Newell, Kevin Moffett, Katrina Dodson, Anelise Chen, Steven Dunn, Molly McGhee, and a truly gnarly amount more. Unfasten the cover, pop open this book's three tubular rings, and unfurl the unruly and radiantly conceived worlds of *McSweeney's 80*.

ONLY SON
by Kevin Moffett

Florida, 1982. A nine-year-old watches as his dead father's possessions are hauled away: his clothes and tools, his faux-leather recliner. His sensei says it's a perfect time to turn his weaknesses into weapons. His PE teacher says he runs like a pregnant ostrich. His mother takes out a personals ad. Everyone is trying to teach him a lesson but he is, it seems, a slow learner. Meanwhile, with each passing day, his father recedes, growing less and less plausible, almost a myth. With wit and compassion, award-winning author Kevin Moffett's debut novel (long-listed for the National Book Award) delivers a bracingly intimate account of fatherhood, and discovery, and the experiences of two men far from home.

MARTHA'S DAUGHTER
by David Haynes

Martha's Daughter is the brilliant and influential author David Haynes's first short story collection and the first time that Haynes's stories have ever been assembled in one volume. Steeped in everyday gossip and lives, this collection ranges from the magically real life of a city's crumbling superhero to a rundown motel whose long-term guests are lucky to call home. In the titular novella the first hours are chronicled after Cynthia finds out her mother has died. What we learn is that Cynthia is a woman who has been bullied by her mother's overbearing opinions, her disdain for difference, her respectability politics, and her outdated beliefs about how men and women should relate to one another. Martha's death is less a catalyst for Cynthia's grief than an opportunity to free herself of a burden too long endured.

PORTHOLE

by Joanna Howard

World-renowned art-house film director Helena Désir may (or may not!) be responsible for the on-set death of Corey, her latest muse, leading man of the moment, and frequent bedmate. Haunted by the accident, a long trail of ex-lovers, and the corporate film studio who desperately wants to keep her, their cash cow, at work, Helena unravels and is swiftly delivered to a luxury retreat known as Jaquith House, where fellow sufferers of psychic exhaustion ferry her from meal, to rest activity, to spa experience, to canoe ride, and back to dinner again, with unmatched hilarity and wit. Hallucinatory and imagistic, filled to the brim with champagne toasts, dressing room hookups, and red carpet faux pas, *Porthole* gifts us the world through the eye of the camera lens, as if through a sea of glass, and asks: If we've sinned in the service of art, can we be forgiven?

AFTER YOU WERE, I AM

by Camille Ralphs

In *After You Were, I Am*, charged moments from history collide with our own godless modern world. The book's three sections—rewritings of canonical prayers, dramatic monologues from the Pendle witch trials of 1612, and the divine tragedy of the Elizabethan magus John Dee—obsess over individual human characters, and how our past informs (and informs on) our present. This is poetry as incantation, plea and invocation. An extraordinary debut from Camille Ralphs, heralding the arrival of a major new talent, this ambitious collection embodies the variety and singularity of living voices past and present, which through rapturous music, anarchic wordplay, and formal distortion are dragged to breaking point.

IF YOU DON'T WANT TO BE PUNCHED, DON'T PUNCH SOMEBODY ELSE: THE LIVES OF CAROLE HINOJOSA

by Carole Hinojosa

After three decades unhoused and addicted in Portland, Oregon, Carole Hinojosa now serves the people she used to live among. With fearless candor, Carole narrates her past, including the circumstances that led her to separate from her young daughter. Ten years after a court order that changed her life, Carole walks us through her days—her tireless advocacy on behalf of people whose lives she understands intimately as well as her reunion with her beloved daughter. The second book in our *Dispatches* series, *If You Don't Want to Be Punched, Don't Punch Somebody Else: The Lives of Carole Hinojosa* provides a vital, timely, and firsthand look into our nation's housing and homelessness crisis.

MOSTLY EVERYTHING: THE ART OF TUCKER NICHOLS

by Tucker Nichols

The first career-spanning book from Bay Area artist Tucker Nichols, *Mostly Everything: The Art of Tucker Nichols* attempts to capture, in one extravagant volume, decades of the artist's varied work, from drawings with words, drawings without words, paintings, and sculpture, to large- and medium-scale public works, editorial illustrations, picture books, doodles, notes, charts, lists, and more. Bound in a luxurious, hard-to-describe double-hardcover book, with two spines and two overlapping cover boards, and clocking in at over three hundred full-color pages, *Mostly Everything: The Art of Tucker Nichols* contains a lifetime of making that can't quite be contained.

LEAVES OF GRASS (DELUXE TWO-VOLUME SET)

by Walt Whitman

Several years in the making, McSweeney's presents a gorgeous cloth-bound, hardcover, two-book edition of *Leaves of Grass*, stuffed to the brim with a dazzling array of ephemera designed to deeply enhance readers' appreciation of Whitman's original masterpiece. Featuring stunning new cover art by Jessica Hische and a slipcase illustrated by Angel Chang. In addition to the original, full-length work (presented precisely as Whitman desired), readers will find a second volume filled with his note-book and manuscript pages—generously made available to us and to all by the Walt Whitman Archive—totaling 344 pages of handwriting, cross outs, substitutions, and notes to both himself and his publishers. These materials provide crucial insight into how this magnificent work was created and was considered and reconsidered over the years by its author.

ROTTEN EVIDENCE

by Ahmed Naji

In February 2016, Ahmed Naji was sentenced to two years in prison for "violating public decency," after an excerpt of his novel *Using Life* reportedly caused a reader to experience heart palpitations. Naji ultimately served ten months of that sentence, in a group cellblock in Cairo's Tora Prison. *Rotten Evidence* is a chronicle of those months. Through Naji's writing, the world of Egyptian prison comes into vivid focus, with its cigarette-based economy, homemade chess sets, and well-groomed fixers. Naji's storytelling is lively and uncompromising, filled with rare insights into both the mundane and grand questions he confronts.

CLOSE QUARTERS

Close Quarters members are a dedicated group of *McSweeney's Quarterly* subscribers who fervently believe that independent publishing is crucial for a culture of free, vibrant expression. Together, we're dedicated to telling the untold stories of our time, and providing readers with a sense of hope and adventure. McSweeney's publishes elegant books and periodicals that capture the complexity of the human experience, and our literary arts programs provide meaningful opportunities for readers, writers, and artists. Close Quarters members are crucial to making our work possible.

Join us. Donate via our online store, or, to learn more, please contact Amanda Uhle at amanda@mcsweeneys.net.

Our heartfelt thanks to these Close Quarters members. They are cherished friends whose support is crucial to the work we do.

Anne Barker
Adam Blanchard
Carli Cutchin
Carol Davis
Brian Dice
Mark Fisher
Brett Goldblatt
Daniel Grossman
Jonathan Huang
Jordan Kurland
Chris Moultrie
Jonathan Parker
Gina & Dave Pell
Douglas Ross
Jed Repko
Sanchia Semere
Jessica Silverman
Alex Tievsky & Jeff Paulatti
Caro Unger
Johanna Wolfe
Cameo Wood

ALSO AVAILABLE FROM McSWEENEY'S

Hannah Versus the Tree .... Leland de la Durantaye
The Comebacker .... Dave Eggers
The Every .... Dave Eggers
A Hologram for the King .... Dave Eggers
The Honor of Your Presence .... Dave Eggers
How We Are Hungry .... Dave Eggers
The Keeper of the Ornaments .... Dave Eggers
The Museum of Rain .... Dave Eggers
The Ocean Is Everyone's but It Is Not Yours .... Dave Eggers
Sanrevelle .... Dave Eggers
Where the Candles Are Kept .... Dave Eggers
The Wild Things .... Dave Eggers
You Shall Know Our Velocity .... Dave Eggers
Donald .... Stephen Elliott, Eric Martin
Painted Cities .... Alexai Galaviz-Budziszewski
A Woman's Place .... Marita Golden
The Boatbuilder .... Daniel Gumbiner
God Says No .... James Hannaham
Martha's Daughter .... David Haynes
The Middle Stories .... Sheila Heti
Porthole .... Joanna Howard
My Favorite Girlfriend Was a French Bulldog .... Legna Rodríguez Iglesias
Pay As You Go .... Eskor David Johnson
Bowl of Cherries .... Millard Kaufman
Misadventure .... Millard Kaufman
Kayfabe .... Chris Koslowski
Lemon .... Lawrence Krauser
The Facts of Winter .... Paul La Farge, Paul Poissel
Search Sweet Country .... Kojo Laing
You People .... Nikita Lalwani
Hot Pink .... Adam Levin
The Instructions .... Adam Levin
Praisesong for the Widow .... Paule Marshall
Only Son .... Kevin Moffett
In Case of Emergency .... Courtney Moreno
Adios, Cowboy .... Olja Savičević
Yr Dead .... Sam Sax
A Moment in the Sun .... John Sayles
Between Heaven and Here .... Susan Straight
The End of Love .... Marcos Giralt Torrente
One Hundred and Forty Five Stories in a Small Box ....
.... Deb Olin Unferth, Sarah Manguso, Dave Eggers
Vacation .... Deb Olin Unferth

The Best of McSweeney's .... Various
Fine, Fine, Fine, Fine, Fine.. Diane Williams
Vicky Swanky Is a Beauty .... Diane Williams
The Fire in His Wake.. Spencer Wolff
My Documents .... Alejandro Zambra

ART AND COMICS

The Portlandia Activity Book...
................Carrie Brownstein, Fred Armisen, Jonathan Krisel; ed. Sam Riley
The Berliner Ensemble Thanks You All .... Marcel Dzama
It Is Right to Draw Their Fur .... Dave Eggers
Binky Brown Meets the Holy Virgin Mary .... Justin Green
Animals of the Ocean, in Particular the Giant Squid...............Dr. and Mr. Doris Haggis-on-Whey
Children and the Tundra ....Dr. and Mr. Doris Haggis-on-Whey
Cold Fusion ....Dr. and Mr. Doris Haggis-on-Whey
Giraffes? Giraffes!.............................Dr. and Mr. Doris Haggis-on-Whey
Celebrations of Curious Characters .... Ricky Jay
There Are Many of Us... Spike Jonze
Mostly Everything .... Tucker Nichols
My Gaza: A City in Photographs................................ Jehad al-Saftawi
Captioning the Archives.......................... Lester Sloan, Aisha Sabatini Sloan
Be a Nose!.. Art Spiegelman
The Clock Without a Face .... Gus Twintig
Everything That Rises: A Book of Convergences................... Lawrence Weschler

BOOKS FOR CHILDREN

Here Comes the Cat! .... Frank Asch; ill. Vladimir Vagin
The Goods ....Eds. Mac Barnett, Brian McMullen
Benny's Brigade .... Arthur Bradford; ill. Lisa Hanawalt
Keep Our Secrets...Jordan Crane
This Bridge Will Not Be Gray .... Dave Eggers; ill. Tucker Nichols
The Eyes and the Impossible .... Dave Eggers; ill. Shawn Harris
The Lights & Types of Ships at Night .... Dave Eggers, ill. Annie Dills
The Night Riders .... Matt Furie
We Need a Horse.. Sheila Heti; ill. Clare Rojas
Stories 1, 2, 3, 4 .... Eugène Ionesco
Hang Glider & Mud Mask.......................... Jason Jägel, Brian McMullen
The Nosyhood.. Tim Lahan
Symphony City.. Amy Martin
Chicken of the Sea................................ Viet Thanh Nguyen; ill. Thi Bui

Crabtree .... Jon and Tucker Nichols
Recipe .... Angela and Michaelanne Petrella; ills. Mike Bertino, Erin Althea
The Defiant .... M. Quint
Awake Beautiful Child .... Amy Krouse Rosenthal; ill. Gracia Lam
Lost Sloth .... J. Otto Seibold
Umbra .... Jordan Speer
The Expeditioners I .... S. S. Taylor; ill. Katherine Roy
The Expeditioners II .... S. S. Taylor; ill. Katherine Roy
Castle on the River Vistula .... Michelle Tea; ill. Kelsey Short
Girl at the Bottom of the Sea .... Michelle Tea; ill. Amanda Verwey
Mermaid in Chelsea Creek .... Michelle Tea; ill. Jason Polan
Noisy Outlaws, Unfriendly Blobs... .... Various

NONFICTION

The Game: A Digital Turning Point .... Alessandro Baricco; trans. Clarissa Botsford
In My Home There Is No More Sorrow .... Rick Bass
Of Color .... Jaswinder Bolina
Maps and Legends .... Michael Chabon
Real Man Adventures .... T Cooper
Information Doesn't Want to Be Free .... Cory Doctorow
The Pharmacist's Mate and 8 .... Amy Fusselman
Toro Bravo: Stories. Recipes. No Bull. .... John Gorham, Liz Crain
Beck's Song Reader .... Beck Hansen
The Strangest of Theatres: Poets Writing Across Borders .... Eds. Jared Hawkley, Susan Rich, Brian Turner
The End of War .... John Horgan
Songbook .... Nick Hornby
Rerun Era .... Joanna Howard
Unnecessarily Beautiful Spaces for Young Minds on Fire .... Ed. The International Alliance of Youth Writing Centers
It Chooses You .... Miranda July
Black Imagination: Black Voices on Black Futures .... Ed. Natasha Marin
Black Powerful: Black Voices Reimagine Revolution .... Ed. Natasha Marin
The End of Major Combat Operations .... Nick McDonell
All That Is Evident Is Suspect: Readings from the Oulipo, 1963–2018 .... Eds. Ian Monk, Daniel Levin Becker
Mission Street Food .... Anthony Myint, Karen Leibowitz
Rotten Evidence .... Ahmed Naji
I Know What's Best for You .... Ed. Shelly Oria
Indelible in the Hippocampus .... Ed. Shelly Oria
Dispatches #1: The Four Deportations of Jean Marseille .... Eds. Peter Orner, Laura Lampton Scott

VOICE OF WITNESS

POETRY

Tombo .... W. S. Di Piero
Morning in Serra Mattu .... Arif Gamal
Flowers of Anti-Martyrdom .... Dorian Geisler
Of Lamb .... Matthea Harvey; ill. Amy Jean Porter
The Abridged History of Rainfall .... Jay Hopler
Still Life .... Jay Hopler
Shadow Act: An Elegy for Journalist James Foley .... Daniel Brock Johnson
Tradition .... Daniel Khalastchi
Love, an Index .... Rebecca Lindenberg
Waders .... Andrew Motion
Fragile Acts .... Allan Peterson
After You Were, I Am .... Camille Ralphs
In the Shape of a Human Body I Am Visiting the Earth ....
.... Various; eds. Ilya Kaminsky, Dominic Luxford, Jesse Nathan
The McSweeney's Book of Poets Picking Poets .... Various; ed. Dominic Luxford
Leaves of Grass .... Walt Whitman

PLAYS

The Domestic Crusaders .... Wajahat Ali
Sorry to Bother You .... Boots Riley

HUMOR

Baby Do My Banking .... Lisa Brown
Baby Fix My Car .... Lisa Brown
Baby Get Me Some Lovin' .... Lisa Brown
Baby Make Me Breakfast .... Lisa Brown
Baby Plan My Wedding .... Lisa Brown
How to Dress for Every Occasion .... Daniel Handler, The Pope
Comedy by the Numbers .... Eric Hoffman, Gary Rudoren
Rosamond Lehmann in Vegas .... Nick Hornby
The Emily Dickinson Reader .... Paul Legault
All Known Metal Bands .... Dan Nelson
A Load of Hooey .... Bob Odenkirk
Welcome to Woodmont College .... Mike Sacks, Jason Roeder
The Latke Who Couldn't Stop Screaming .... Lemony Snicket; ill. Lisa Brown
The Secret Language of Sleep .... Evany Thomas; ill. Amelia Bauer
I Found This Funny .... Various; ed. Judd Apatow
The Future Dictionary of America ....
.. Various; eds. Jonathan Safran Foer, Dave Eggers, Nicole Krauss, Eli Horowitz
I Live Real Close to Where You Used to Live .... Various; ed. Lauren Hall
Thanks and Have Fun Running the Country .... Various; ed. Jory John

Keep Scrolling Till You Feel Something .... Various; eds. Chris Monks, Sam Riley
The Best of McSweeney's Internet Tendency. Various; eds. Chris Monks, John Warner

COLLINS LIBRARY

Curious Men .... Frank Buckland
The Lunatic at Large .... J. Storer Clouston
English as She Is Spoke .... José da Fonseca; Pedro Carolino
Lady into Fox .... David Garnett
The Riddle of the Traveling Skull .... Harry Stephen Keeler
The Rector and the Rogue .... W. A. Swanberg

Founded in 1998, McSweeney's is an independent publisher based in San Francisco. McSweeney's exists to champion ambitious and inspired new writing, and to challenge conventional expectations about where it's found, how it looks, and who participates. We're here to discover things we love, help them find their most resplendent form, and place them into the hands of curious, engaged readers.

THERE ARE SEVERAL WAYS TO SUPPORT MCSWEENEY'S:

Support Us on Patreon
visit *www.patreon.com/mcsweeneysinternettendency*

Subscribe & Shop
visit *store.mcsweeneys.net*

Volunteer & Intern
email *contact@mcsweeneys.net*

Sponsor Books & Periodicals
email *amanda@mcsweeneys.net*

To learn more, please visit *www.mcsweeneys.net/donate* or contact Executive Director Amanda Uhle at *amanda@mcsweeneys.net* or 415.642.5609.

McSweeney's Literary Arts Fund is a nonprofit organization as described by IRS 501(c)(3). Your support is invaluable to us.